D0205615

LIBRARY WORK
WITH
CHILDREN

LIBRARY WORK
WITH
CHILDREN

*With special reference to
developing countries*

BY

LEONARD MONTAGUE
HARROD

GRAFTON BASIC TEXTS
Editor: Evelyn J. A. Evans, C.B.E., F.L.A.

A GRAFTON BOOK

ANDRE DEUTSCH

FIRST PUBLISHED 1969 BY
ANDRE DEUTSCH LIMITED
105 GREAT RUSSELL STREET
LONDON WC1
COPYRIGHT © 1969 BY L. M. HARROD
ALL RIGHTS RESERVED
PRINTED IN GREAT BRITAIN BY
C. TINLING & CO LTD
LIVERPOOL, LONDON AND PRESCOT
SBN 233 95994 7

CONTENTS

LIST OF PLATES

LIST OF FIGURES

PREFACE

The provision of libraries for children has always been one of my chief interests, for the first article I wrote on a professional subject was entitled "The Future of the Children's Library" and appeared in the *Library Assistant* in 1926. This book is the result of that interest, and not of my present occupation, as I do not lecture on this subject except in so far as the planning and furnishing of libraries impinges on library work with children.

The first draft was written while working in Singapore where I realised how much untrained or inexperienced librarians were in need of guidance. It is mainly for such readers that this book should be of most use, for it deals with the fundamentals of children's libraries; but in addition, it covers the provision of a comprehensive service for children in public libraries.

Classification and cataloguing are mentioned only briefly, and school libraries sketchily, because these are the subjects of other books in the Grafton Basic Texts Series.

I am grateful to those who have provided photographs, and to my former colleague, Charles A. Elliott, for lending items for photographing, to the Editor of *Education Libraries Bulletin* and Miss P. M. Cadge for permission to reproduce part of her thesis printed in that periodical, and also to Miss Elizabeth Haines, Dip. AD who made the drawings.

A*

'But there was something more, and here he could quote Dr Johnson more specifically to his purpose. "Have as many books about you as you can," he told Boswell, "I am always for getting a boy forward in his learning; for that is a sure good. I would let him read *any* English book which happens to engage his attention; because you have done a great deal when you have brought him to have entertainment from a book. He'll get better books afterwards!"

' "I would put a child into a library (where no unfit books are) and let him read at his choice. A child should not be discouraged from reading anything that he takes a liking to, from a notion that it is above his reach." '

BOSWELL'S Life of Johnson

CHAPTER I

Fundamentals and Provision of a Children's Library Service

THE CHILDREN'S NEED FOR READING MATTER

Parents usually have books or magazines lying about in their home, and their small children consequently get used to seeing such reading matter as part of their home furnishings. The sensible mother who is anxious that her children's mental and cultural development, as well as their physical development, will take place, introduces her small children to books as soon as they show an interest in them. This they do at the age of about two to three years. Although children cannot read at this age, and are not usually able to do so until four or five years of age, there are many simple books consisting mainly of illustrations but with a few words relating to the illustrations on each page, which can be shown to the children while the stories are being read to them. In this way the children associate words with the pictures, and when they are able to identify letters forming the words, they will be able to read these stories for themselves.

When they are able to read with a fair amount of ease, they will themselves want to read rather than be read to (although they will still enjoy this form of relaxed 'reading') and they will want to read frequently. Many newly literate older children are just as anxious to have books as soon as they have learned to read as children who come from literate backgrounds who learned to read at a very early age.

Children of average intelligence and ability become avid readers at about seven or eight providing they have learnt to read at about five; and for approximately three years they will want to spend much of their spare time reading. This is apparently a natural inclination and is one which should be encouraged and fostered. It is necessary, however, that children of this age have access to good quality books. It would be unwise to let them see nothing but comics or reading matter of poor quality.

It is essential for a child's educational and cultural development to ensure that a good supply of excellent and appropriate books is available. If children do not have such books to read, they will – because they must read *something* – fall back on whatever comes to hand, and this may be reading matter which their parents and their teachers would not wish them to have.

Years of experience observing the reading habits and social characteristics of children who are able to read easily and make good use of a library shows that, quite apart from anything else, children who are good readers, and read widely, are usually those who manage to pass examinations whilst at school with more ease than the children who have not yet learned the art of reading for pleasure. These children enlarge their experience of the world about them and of foreign countries and the things which are not normally within a child's experience or education. They are also much better able to express themselves clearly in writing because they are used to the sequence of words and ideas in the books they have read.

Kinds of Library Service
Apart from books which are to be found in the home there are two main sources of books. These are (a) public libraries and (b) school libraries.

Public libraries. Public library services should be financed entirely from public funds, whether these are government funds or local authority funds. It is the world-wide policy of UNESCO that all libraries should be free, and many countries with progressive library services make no charges for the use of the library, the sources of income being the national or local exchequer.

There should be no barriers, either of race or of creed, to the use of the library and it should be open to people of all ages, even to the child who, although unable to read, can appreciate simple books when they are read to him. If he is unable to sign his name on an application card for membership of the library, but his parents are willing to borrow books for him and in his name, then he should be entitled to become a library member, his parents signing the application form on his behalf.

These public library services can be provided either in static libraries – that is those which are placed in a building – or from mobile libraries. Static libraries are the most usual form of library provision, although they are not so economical as mobile libraries unless the expenditure on their erection and maintenance is justified by their being in continuous use by large numbers of people. Static libraries tie up capital in the form of buildings for which rates and taxes, and cleaning, staffing and maintenance costs, have to be paid. It is not usual therefore to provide static libraries until demand justifies opening for most of each day. This demand can be assessed, not so much by frequent requests for a library service, as by testing the use which is likely to be made of a library, by supplying books by means of a deposit station (that is a building at which books are deposited for two or three months and then changed), or in rented premises, or by allowing a mobile library to stop in the vicinity for several hours each week or each fortnight. Where demand is not great enough to keep a mobile library busy for twenty hours a week it is certainly not economical to provide a static library.

Static libraries usually contain books for home reading by adults and children, and also small collections of works of reference, which may not be taken home but must be referred to on the premises. Reference books are those which are compiled to be referred to for specific information, not to be read through. Of such are dictionaries, gazetteers, encyclopaedias, atlases and year books.

Readers must be free to choose the books they want to read, but it is advisable to have on duty at every library service point a member of the staff with sufficient knowledge and experience of library work and also of the stock, to be able to guide the readers in their choice of books. Once a varied and unbiased stock has been placed on the shelves there should be no direction as to its use, but only suggestive guidance as to the most suitable books for individual readers; this guidance should not be forced upon the readers but be available whenever it is requested.

The stock of books for children should consist of story books and books of information (normally called non-fiction books by librarians) for home-reading and also a selection of suitable reference books. The books supplied, the methods of issuing them and arranging them on the shelves, the general administration of the library and its objectives should all be similar to those of the adult library. The children's library should serve as an introduction to the adult library as well as meet the children's immediate desire for reading matter.

The extent to which a government may supervise the provision of public libraries by local authorities may be seen in the Public Libraries and Museums Act, 1964, the new legislation for which British librarians had been waiting for many years. For the first time, a member of the Government has a specific responsibility for library services, it being the 'duty of the Secretary of State to superintend, and promote the improvement of, the public library service provided by local authorities in England and Wales, and to secure the proper discharge by local authorities of the functions in relation to libraries conferred on them as library authorities . . .' (I(I)). Also, for the first time, a standard of service is mentioned in library legislation, as follows: 'It shall be the duty of every library authority to provide a comprehensive and efficient library service for all persons desiring to make use thereof, and for that purpose to employ such officers, to provide and maintain such buildings and equipment, and such books and other materials, and to do such other things, as may be requisite . . .' In fulfilling this duty 'a library authority shall in particular have regard to the desirability – (a) of securing, by the keeping of adequate stocks, by arrangements with other library authorities, and by any other appropriate means, that facilities are available for the borrowing of, or reference to, books and other printed matter, and pictures, gramophone records, films and other materials, sufficient in number, range and quality to meet the general requirements and any special requirements both of adults and children; and (b) of encouraging both adults and children to make full use of the library service . . .' (s. 7 (1) and (2)). The Introduction to the Roberts Report[1] (of the Committee set up by the Minister of Education in September 1957 under the chairmanship of Sir Sydney Roberts 'to consider the structure of the public library service in England and Wales, and to advise what changes, if any, should be made in the administrative arrangements, regard being had to the relation of public libraries to other libraries') states that 'the function of the public library is not only to satisfy, but to promote the desire for books. Consequently the provision of a children's library with adequate stocks and expert guidance in the choice of books should be regarded as an integral part of the library service'. This Roberts Report[1] was the first formal stage in preparations leading to the new legislation. A later stage was the Report[2] of the Working Party, of which Mr H. T. Bourdillon of the Ministry

---

[1] *The structure of the public library service in England and Wales.* 1959.
[2] *Standards of public library service in England and Wales; report of the Working Party appointed by the Minister of Education in March 1961.*

of Education was Chairman. In stating the objectives and functions of the public library service it commented that all libraries should make special provision for children and should do all they can to ensure that children are encouraged to use the library. They should also endeavour to cater for the special needs of young adults[1]. One of the factors affecting the efficiency of a library service was considered to be 'the maintenance of a high standard of quality [of children's books provided], both as regards content and condition [and that this] is more important than the coverage of a wide range of the books published'. The Working Party considered 'that every library providing a basic library service should buy annually not less than 1,500 volumes of children's books. This would mean the purchase of some 750 titles, equivalent to one-third of all the children's books published annually in this country'.[2] The Report enumerated services such as those mentioned in the section on extension work, which supplement and complement the provision of books and added: 'We consider that library work with children is an important part of public library service which calls for specially trained staff both at central and at major branch libraries'.[3] It will be appreciated that these quotations relate to a country with well-developed library services; the fundamental theory is applicable in any country, however.

Another branch of public libraries' provision for children is concerned with a service to schools as distinct from providing school libraries. This is referred to in the Working Party's report as follows:[4]

'Most of the larger municipal libraries and all the county libraries in our survey provided books for schools

---

[1] *Op. cit.* para. 18   [2] *Op. cit.* para. 47
[3] *Op. cit.* para. 77   [4] *Op. cit.* para. 79.

16

on behalf of the education authority. The larger authorities, particularly county libraries, maintained permanent exhibitions of the best children's books in print to assist teachers in the selection of books for school libraries. The service provided to schools (which was not limited to libraries receiving a grant for their services) included talks in schools and to parent-teacher associations, instruction in library use to visiting parties of school children, the provision of lists of outstanding children's books, the loan of collections of material (including illustrations) for school projects, and the provision of special library facilities for teachers. Two county boroughs had joint education-library sub-committees to secure effective liaison between the two departments. It is apparent that both schools and public libraries stand to gain if there is effective liaison between the two services, whether or not the public library acts as an agency for the provision of school library books. This agency service, which normally supplements books held permanently by schools, seems to us an administratively useful arrangement.'

School libraries. It is now generally accepted that every school catering for children of four or five years of age upwards i.e. primary (infants and junior) and secondary schools, should have its own library. Every school should contain books appropriate to the ages of the children attending, and should provide, unless a branch of a public library is very close to the school, fiction and non-fiction books which can be read as supplements to the subjects which are studied in class. In the primary school a small library is usually placed in each class-room but there should be a central library within the school catering for the children as a whole and also containing reference books for consultation on the premises.

Where there is a public library nearby there is a duplication of effort if the school also provides books for home reading. Yet the provision of a school library is often the most effective means of ensuring that *all* children are encouraged to use books – providing that the books in it are suitable, up-to-date, adequate in number and content, and also that the staff are keen enough, and able, to direct the children to use the library intelligently. Children should be encouraged to use the public library for recreational reading matter, and also for books of information, because it is only by developing the habit of using a library not associated with a school that children realize that a library may be not only a part of an educational institution, but that it has something to offer them throughout their lives; they will then tend to go to it with pleasure and independence.

In the smallest school, especially a primary school, it may not be necessary to have very many reference books, but in a large primary school, and certainly in a secondary school, it is essential to have a collection of books which can be referred to by teachers and pupils at all times whenever information is required. It is particularly important that reference books should be provided in a room reserved for that purpose in schools where children are encouraged to do independent work, such as projects, without constant supervision or direction by the teacher. Experience has shown that even children in primary schools can benefit very largely from using the reference books in a public library for such purposes. The use of books in this way is an extremely important part of children's educational training and should be taught in a school if it is at all possible. If it is not, then recourse should be made to the children's department of the local public library where facilities will be made available – probably most readily – to the children to undertake work of this kind during school hours.

Children should learn to appreciate books as a means of

spending their free time pleasantly as well as for finding information and instruction.

Responsibility for provision

It has already been mentioned that public libraries should be provided from public funds. The reason for this recommendation is that the library so provided is much more likely to be of a permanent nature and of a higher standard than if the library is dependent upon voluntary subscriptions, the subscriptions of members of the library, or the sometimes changing, and often apathetic, views of the committee of a voluntary educational, cultural or social organization or society.

If voluntary subscriptions are the source of income then it means that a number of people have to undertake 'efforts' and 'schemes' every year of the library's existence in order to raise the necessary funds. This means that someone, and inevitably the librarian to some extent, has to whip up considerable interest in order to raise the required money. A paid organizer would avoid all the effort needed on the part of librarian and volunteers, and would probably be more effective. It would, however, result in a considerable expenditure of part of the voluntary subscriptions, but this is inevitable with all large charitable and voluntary organizations of this kind.

The days of patronage by the nobility, or even the wealthy, and of successful subscription societies, are over. If the library is dependent on the subscriptions of its members it is not likely to be a very important or useful institution, largely because it is generally expected that the State should provide educational, cultural, social and health amenities; in these days the library has to be an exceptional and really good one in order to secure the continued patronage of subscribing members, and such a library usually costs more than it is possible to raise by subscriptions. If a subscription library is not good, people will not join, and consequently there will be a smaller amount of money with which to buy books, redecorate the building, refurnish it, pay the salaries of the staff, etc.

Where the source of income is assured and where a public authority is responsible for providing a service it is much more likely that the service so provided will be of a higher standard, will be more likely to meet the needs of the people requiring it, and will be staffed by qualified and experienced librarians who are more likely to make a success of the library than unqualified persons employed by a committee whose income depends on voluntary subscriptions or the subscriptions of members.

The source of income ought not to affect very materially the type of library service provided, although it can easily be foreseen that a library which is not provided from public funds may have no children's department, or no reference library, or that the service which is provided is inadequate in some respects. Where money is limited and cannot be increased, then the services provided must be curtailed accordingly.

Of what should the children's library service consist?

A public library service for children should consist of (a) books for home-reading, (b) reading-room facilities, and (c) books for reference.

The provision of books for home reading is the most important aspect of the public library service; it is the one which is used more than any other by members of the public, and it is one which is likely to have a very much wider and more lasting influence on the members of the community.

Reading-room facilities vary considerably from place to place and also from one country to another. There are however important reasons in certain countries, particularly in the under-developed countries, for providing reading-rooms. Many homes are hopelessly overcrowded and congested, and also lighting conditions, both in the day-time and also at night, are very inadequate. In many places, neither electricity nor high-pressure oil-lamps are available. If a reading-room can be provided where people who live in such uncongenial housing conditions can go and read periodicals, newspapers or books, an important social and educational service is being provided.

The third form of library service is the reference library. It is not only necessary to provide an adequate supply of the right kind of books to meet the needs of the public but also to provide staff. Assistants in adult reference libraries need a particular approach to this kind of work; they must have an inherent interest in things in general and an inquisitive type of mind; they must also have a facility for ferreting out information and for being patient, not giving up should they be unable to find easily what they are seeking. It is an advantage if they are among the more experienced members of the staff, because successful reference library work depends very largely on the accumulated knowledge of the contents of books, which, although this can be learned consciously and purposefully, is also assimilated with experience over the years. Such knowledge cannot be obtained very quickly and certainly not without some conscious effort. Although the demands on a reference library service in a children's library are not likely to be very great, these qualities are necessary in a children's librarian. It is important that children in any children's library, even the smallest, should be given sympathetic, helpful and informed assistance with their requests for information.

Where should the children's library be placed?
The children's library should be as near as possible to the children's homes and it should be in a building used exclusively for the purposes of the library if it is an urban area.

In a rural or semi-urban area, a building used for general cultural, educational or social health purposes is suitable. Although shared buildings are often satisfactory, the library service should, whenever possible, be provided as a completely autonomous service and not part of any other.

STAFFING THE CHILDREN'S LIBRARY

The first essential for an efficient and effective library service is to have an adequate supply of good books; the second is to have a technically competent and otherwise suitable staff to exploit the books and see that they are used to the best advantage. The quality of the library work, the use of the adult library in the future when the children become too old for the junior library, and the standards of behaviour of persons using the adult library, all depend largely on the quality of the work carried out in the children's library and the way in which the children are trained to be library users. This training depends almost entirely on the quality of the children's library staff and the work they do.

What are the good qualities that should be looked for in a children's librarian? She should have a liking for children; she should try to understand them, and be interested in them and their activities; she should know what children like to read and what children are capable of reading at different ages; she should discover all she can that appertains to children's interests, to their ways, habits, thoughts, and interests. Librarians working with children need, even more than other librarians, a sense of vocation. The work is not easy, because sometimes children, particularly if there are many of them milling round in the library at the same time, can cause commotion, and disrupt the peaceful usage of the library. The librarian must be capable of working hard physically as well as mentally, and must be able to undertake very tiring work for periods of two or three hours at a stretch when a busy library is inundated with children.

The librarian's interests should not however, be limited to children and to the work of the children's library. She should have an interest in all branches of library work and should consider her work with children merely as part, but a very important part, of the library's work as a whole. She should like her own work and must create an atmosphere of happiness and pleasure so that children will feel that the children's library is a happy and pleasant place in which to be. A children's librarian needs to cultivate an awareness of everything that is going on, her ears, eyes, and other senses being constantly on the alert; she must be aware of what children are doing when they are in the library, even without consciously observing them. She needs to find out how they are behaving with quick side-long glances cast over the whole of the children's library, when looking from one place to another. If she is discharging books, she must not merely be aware of the child standing in front of her and the book she is discharging, she must be aware of what else is going on in the room, and have her mind on all the activities which are being undertaken.

She will find that some children will try to get the better of her, outwitting her in securing favours, possibly trying to get books to which they are not entitled, hiding books so that they will be in a hidden place ready for them (or for their friends) the next time they come in, and she must be aware of pranks and mischievousness which the children may get up to. She should anticipate their behaviour, and if she suspects that misbehaviour is going to develop, must try to prevent it. She should know how the children ought to behave and she must see that they behave in this way. She must run the department with a firm but kindly hand, making sure that none of the children takes advantage of her in any way.

In other words, she needs to be a good disciplinarian, making sure that they do not misbehave; and she will have to do this by herself without the assistance of a male attendant ('caretaker', 'janitor', 'porter', or whatever he is called) who should not be permitted to control the children's behaviour in the children's library. He should be required to comply with her authority on the rare occasion when a child needs to be shown out of the building as a punishment for misbehaviour, and only then if the child is unwilling to go when requested. She should herself create an atmosphere of quiet and orderliness in behaviour and in movement.

In outlook she should be as young as the children themselves, but with the maturity necessary to maintain order and to see that their legitimate needs are supplied. She needs to get to know her members as individuals – not to look upon them merely as people coming to the library for a book, but fellow human beings with a common interest. It is therefore advisable for her to cultivate a friendliness with them which can best be expressed in a welcoming smile, constant politeness, and, when time permits, conversation with them at their own level on things which interest them.

What sort of person makes a good children's librarian? Primarily and fundamentally one who is friendly, a good mixer, of sound character and having much commonsense; she must be patient, not easily put out by misbehaviour or pressure of work, remaining calm at all times; she must like children and be tolerant of them and their ways and also of her colleagues; she must be willing to turn her hand to any job that needs to be done in the department even if it is normally done by people junior to herself. It is also an advantage for her to be fairly good at handicrafts and also at simple pen lettering so that she can make notices for the library quickly and satisfactorily; she should also be practically minded and able to use her hands in the performance of her manual duties with skill and speed. Above all, she must possess and develop an interest in children's books, being willing to read – or at least sample – all the new ones, otherwise she cannot guide the children in their choice of books.

A person who is to take charge of a children's library should be professionally competent, having passed *at least* the intermediate examination of a professional association, and also any additional examinations in library work with children. It is essential that she should be fully competent professionally because otherwise she will be unable to make decisions which require professional knowledge, or see that her department functions efficiently, not only as an independent unit but also as part of the complete library service. She will also, in a larger library, doubtless have younger assistants to help her, and these will need guidance, instruction and training. This she would have difficulty in doing without being fully trained and qualified herself.

RULES FOR USING THE LIBRARY

Every organization must have rules for its satisfactory running, and a library is no exception. They must (a) define the persons who are entitled to use it, (b) lay down the conditions of such usage, (c) protect the building and its contents against malicious and accidental damage, and (d) prescribe any penalties for non-compliance with the rules.

Rules are often extremely useful to refer to in order to back up a librarian's action in maintaining discipline or justifying an action which is normal routine but which is objected to, or questioned, by a member – in fact this is, in actual practice, their chief use. This necessity does not arise so often in a junior library as in an adult library, but they are nevertheless very useful sometimes in dealing with parents. The whole code of library practice is built up within the framework of the rules, and although intending members should have an opportunity of reading the rules when they join the library it is not necessary to print them and give them to the members: a brief description of the services and facilities available is much more acceptable and more useful.

The rules for a children's library need not be as elaborate as those for an adult library. Where a children's library is part of a larger library, many of the provisions such as those relating to (c) and possibly (d) above would be included in the main rules which would in fact apply to the whole of the organization except where the children's library's conditions and circumstances differed from those of other departments. They should be clearly and briefly expressed in simple words; they should be positive whenever possible and not negative.

Rules should be framed in as general terms as possible so that changes in the library service with regard to times of opening, period of loan, fines, etc., may be varied as necessary without having to alter the rules. This is usually achieved by making reference to decisions made by the librarian or the committee from time to time.

The early rules should state clearly who may join the library, either to borrow books, or to consult books, newspapers or magazines. The place of consultation such as a reference library or magazine room need not be mentioned as it is possible that the materials may not always be kept in the same place as when the rules were drawn up.

It is usual, and advisable, for the rules to stipulate that applicants for borrowing books for home reading should live in a specified geographical area in which the library is situated, or otherwise be able to comply with some other condition such as attendance at a school in such an area. Those who normally live in another area but have no connexion with the area providing the library may be entitled to join on paying a deposit which is returnable when membership of the library ceases, or on presenting a ticket issued by another library, or by paying a subscription. Persons who reside temporarily in the area should be enabled to join on having the usual application card signed as if they were permanent residents. By having few restrictions in this way, it becomes easy for anyone to use the library.

Age

Although a librarian wishes to know the age of members, age is no bar to membership and need not be referred to in the rules. If for some reason, such as shortage of books in general, or of books for small children, it is necessary to restrict membership, this may be done by having a lower age limit; but any such restriction is best avoided. There is no need to mention an upper age limit. If it is anticipated that an age limit may at some time have to be imposed or removed, a general reference to ages 'such as the committee may from time to time determine' is satisfactory. Any normal child will wish to transfer to the adult library when he feels he is ready to do so; an age limit presupposes that when a child reaches a certain age he is sufficiently developed in reading ability or in general knowledge and intelligence to be able to benefit from membership of an adult library. This is an irrational presupposition.

Liability

The rules will require that the parent or the guardian will sign the card and that the head teacher of the school will also sign.

Librarians maintain that a teacher cannot be held financially responsible for books damaged or lost by children, but parents should be expected to make such payments, for someone must be responsible for the proper care of children's books, particularly now that they are so expensive. A sense of civic responsibility should be developed in children – in adults, too, sometimes – and the proper care of library books with enforcible penalties when necessary is an opportunity for doing this. In any case allowance is made for accidents in case of damage or loss, and for wear and tear (taking into consideration the length of time the book had been in stock and its probable condition), when determining a charge – and the full cost is never charged.

The parent's signature would be an undertaking to be responsible for the safe-keeping of the books borrowed, and the teacher's that the applicant was (a) a person to whom the books could be safely lent and (b) likely to benefit from using the library. The exact purpose of each signature, and the degree of responsibility of the signatory, is indicated by the wording on the application card.

There are several advantages in having the teacher endorse the card: he knows which children are using the library and can be a useful ally of the librarian in securing new members; he knows the children and the homes from which they come and could refuse to sign if he felt that the applicant would not benefit from using the library because he was too retarded mentally or for some other reason, or that the parent would not fulfil the obligations entered into. Such co-operation between teacher and librarian would result in the teacher being more willing to help secure the return of overdue books, and he would become more informed about, and more interested in, the work of the library because of more frequent library contacts. He would also be more inclined to further the work of the library amongst his pupils because of his greater awareness of the library's stock, facilities and services, and consequently more inclined to participate in the extension activities mentioned in the section on extension work.

Fines

Should children (or adults for that matter) pay fines for

keeping books beyond the period allowed for reading them? The payment of fines dates back to the early days of public libraries when book funds were low and the additional income was very useful; the number of books available was not as great as it is now, and (in theory) more books could be bought with the extra money. It is true, of course, that such income does not normally go directly into the funds of the library but into the general funds of the local authority or government providing the library service, but it undoubtedly has its influence on those responsible for providing funds for the library, and one hopes these people are consequently more inclined to allow the librarian the little extra for books that he is constantly needing – and quite rightly needing, seeing that the cost of books is constantly rising. These two conditions, shortage of money and of books, still exist in most libraries – not many libraries have enough money to buy all the books they need, or have so good a selection on the shelves that any reader can find what he wants whenever he goes into the library. This last should be the service ideal that any librarian should always have in mind.

Some librarians consider that a system of fines is desirable in order to keep books circulating quickly: there is some truth in this argument. One has known children who were members of a non-public library who were allowed to borrow as many books as they liked, borrowing one or more each week without bothering to return those they already had out and which they had obviously finished reading, or had not read at all. This can be prevented if the number of books members may have out at a time is controlled by limiting the number of tickets they may have and also the number of books allowed on each ticket, as is done in the Browne book charging system. There is no such control with the photographic (and some other) methods of recording loans, and in some libraries overdue notices are not sent out until books are about ten weeks overdue. This means that a larger stock is needed to provide the selection of titles considered desirable, and this results in the tying up of capital to a greater extent than would be the case if books were returned sooner. Should this be a capital charge, or should not readers pay something for keeping books longer than the time allowed and thereby preventing other readers from borrowing them?

It can be argued that to fine a child creates hardship. It may do if the amount levied is high or if the child keeps the book out so long that the total amount exceeds the value of the book. The mere fact that a fine has to be paid may result in some children ceasing to use the library on their own accord because they prefer to use their money for other purposes, or because their parents object. This is one of those barriers to membership which should not exist. If fines are not charged, what can be done to see that books are returned in time? Admonition, pointing out how unsatisfactory a member of society the borrower is by not returning his book on time and so depriving other members of it, is the usual course, but the assistant should enquire in a kindly manner why the book was kept overdue before deciding on the admonition. It may have been because the book was unsuitable for the particular borrower, or because he was a slow reader, or because he was for some good reason unable to get to the library to return it – or there may have been some other quite justifiable reason. Admonition would then be unkind (and worse than a fine), and a word of warning, of suggestion, or even of help in choosing more suitable books which the child could read quickly, would be much more appropriate. If a member were frequently to keep his books overdue, then the tickets could be impounded for a few weeks. This incidentally, might be a more effective deterrent to some readers than charging a fine.

If fines are charged all that the rules need state is that the borrower would be required to pay 'such fines for the retention of books beyond the time allowed for reading them as may be demanded', or 'such fines as may from time to time be levied'; they can then be varied or discontinued at will.

Behaviour
Provision is necessary in the rules to empower the children's librarian to eject from the library, or exclude, any member who misbehaves, and if this is included in the main rules, providing they are phrased to refer to all departments, there is no need to repeat it in the rules relating to the children's library. Such action however should never be necessary, and the need for it could not arise if the library were adequately staffed and the children trained to behave well, as they can be by proper supervision, and admonition when necessary. Friendliness should characterize the staff's relationship with the children, but there must also be firmness in handling them when misbehaviour occurs or a disturbance threatens. An appeal to the children for good behaviour in their library and for the comfort, pleasure and convenience for all users should meet a favourable response from them, but when it does not, the rules (which need only be in general terms) should strengthen the librarians in any action taken.

Property
The necessity for clean hands, and for protecting books, the building, and its furniture and fittings, against damage, should be stated in general terms.

Period allowed for reading
The rules may refer in general terms to a period of loan or may state the number of days allowed for reading the books. The former is preferable as this allows the period to be

altered without the need to alter the rules. They may also include provision for the renewal of loans.

The following is a set of rules suitable for a children's library.

Using the Children's Library
Rules for the guidance of readers

General

Please:

1 Move about the library rooms noiselessly. Talk quietly. Help to keep the room clean and tidy by putting books away when you have finished with them and pushing your chair up to the table.

2 Treat the furniture, the books and the walls of the building carefully, never doing anything to them that would spoil or harm them; to do so would mean that other boys and girls would get less pleasure out of using the library than you do.

3 Do whatever you are told to do by the children's librarian, or any other member of the staff, at once and without question.

4 Always have clean hands when using library books.

The children's librarian or another member of the staff shall have power to refuse the use of the library to any child who does not obey the following rules:

Lending Library

5 Any child residing in, or attending a day-school in
.... may borrow books for home reading on completing the form of application and having it signed by the head teacher of the school attended and also by the parent or guardian.

6 Children who are not so entitled to join may become members on paying an annual subscription the amount of

which may be determined from time to time by the Library Committee, and obtaining the signature of a rate-payer of .... in the place of the head teacher.

7 One book may be borrowed on each ticket issued, and the books are issued for 15 days including days of issue and return, or for such period as may from time to time be determined.

8 Fines at rates to be determined from time to time must be paid on any books kept longer than the period allowed. Alternatively, the tickets may be suspended for a period to be determined by the children's librarian.

9 Books must not be lent to other people.

10 Tickets, which remain the property of the library, are issued to members whose applications are approved. These tickets must not be lent or given to other people.

11 No book may be taken from the library until the loan has been recorded by the children's librarian.

12 Books may be renewed for a further period if they are brought to the library for renewal, and providing they have not been reserved by another reader.

13 Books should be protected from damage by rain when taking them from and to the library. (Protective wrapping will be provided on request.)

14 A book-marker should be used to mark your place; do not turn down the corners of pages or write on them. A charge may be levied at the discretion of the children's librarian in respect of books which may be damaged or lost while on loan.

15 Books which have been exposed to infectious disease must not be returned to the Library but returned to . . .

Reference Library

16 A tracing may only be made after first obtaining a sheet of transparent protective material from the children's librarian.

17 No book may be taken from the Library.

THE CARE OF BOOKS

Books are often damaged by careless handling, and children should be taught formally (in groups when classes come from a school to join the library or to undertake project work) how to handle books without harming them. Other opportunities can be made to give such instruction, as for example when children happen to be joining the library in a group, as often occurs at the beginning of a new school term when they come as a result of encouragement from teachers.

The children's librarian will find other opportunities during the course of her work to give advice or instruction on specific aspects of book-care.

Opening
Sometimes new books have rather tight backs and one hears a crack if they are opened forcibly. Although books should not reach the shelves in an un-eased state, some may do so, and in any case it is useful for children to know how to open a book properly in order that they may not damage their own books.

General care in use
Children should be told to protect books against:
> *damage by heat,* caused by reading too close to a fire or leaving them in the sun;
> *damage by rain,* this can be prevented by carrying them to and from the library in rainy weather in a case or bag, or wrapping them in paper. (Many libraries have a supply of brown paper handy to give readers who are in the library when a shower or storm occurs. In some libraries a small notice is placed on the counter-top where the books are issued advising readers of this);
> *damage by moisture,* caused especially in hot climates by perspiring hands; this can be prevented by putting a cover of brown paper on them;

damage by dirt, prevented to some extent by seeing that hands are clean when in the library, and by not leaving books in dirty places;

damage by dogs, especially puppies;

damage by leaning on open books, or piling other books on them when open;

damage by placing open books face downwards;

damage by throwing books down instead of carefully putting them away when finished with;

damage by turning down the corners of pages to mark a place;

damage by moistening the fingers when turning over pages, or turning them over by pushing up the bottom of the leaf with the thumb, especially near the spine, and thus breaking the paper fibres. A page should be turned by gently separating it at the top right-hand corner with the fingers.

Children should also be told not to use books as teapot or tumbler stands, and not to write or draw on the margins or endpapers.

Any damage which is noticed by children should be reported to the librarian so that a note of it can be made in the book to avoid questioning subsequent borrowers about it.

If damage often occurs, it is a good idea to arrange in a glass case a display of books which have been damaged, especially if a note of any fines which have been levied can be affixed, together with descriptive and admonitory notices, as a means of publicity and prevention.

ASSISTANCE TO READERS

The most important thing which a children's librarian can do after acquiring the books and carrying out the necessary routines in order to make them easily and readily accessible, is to help the children find the reading material or information they require. This aspect of library work has in recent years been called 'assistance to readers'. The giving of any help or information which members require comes under this heading.

The staff in the children's library should always be available to give such help and should be ready to do so. It is as well if the staff can give the impression of being unhurried and always at the children's disposal, ready and anxious to render any assistance they require. Generally speaking, it is not advisable to make a practice of offering such assistance, although it is a good idea to give such help without it appearing to be done obtrusively. If the children's librarian cultivates a friendly attitude towards the children and they learn to trust her and to respect her as someone they can go to for considerate attention, whatever their request may be, then she will find that the children will have no hesitation in approaching her for assistance whenever they need it. She needs to have a full knowledge of the book stock, not only of the authors and titles of the books, but also of their contents.

A children's librarian should not be so tied up with routine work at the staff enclosure that she has no opportunity of helping children without having to neglect several others who are waiting to have books issued or discharged. Such conditions indicate under-staffing. She should always be ready and willing to attend to a child's particular needs, even if this means interrupting her routine work. Children should be encouraged to hold the view that their requests for books or information can be made without causing her the least annoyance, resentment or perturbation, and this attitude can best be developed by the assistant always being ready with a smile and a pleasant manner to welcome requests and deal with them cheerfully. She should never 'snap' at a child but she must know how to be firm with any children who are likely to take advantage of her friendliness, or of her being busy. Noisiness, horseplay, or even useless and aimless occupation of the children's library should not be tolerated.

One of the most important aspects of children's library

work is organized co-operation with the local schools whereby classes attend the library so that the children can undertake individual project study. Experience has shown that this is not only one of the most valuable ways of teaching children to work on their own, and to find out information for themselves and write it up; it is also one of the best means of ensuring that children develop the habit of using the library – and this, after all, is one of the librarian's chief concerns.

A children's librarian should therefore encourage teachers to take children in class groups to the library. It is necessary to obtain from the teacher a list of subjects which the children will be studying and also any particular books which the teacher will wish the children to use. Then, before the classes begin to come to the library, she will make sure that she has the necessary books in her own stock or arrange to obtain them from other departments in the library system. If the children come regularly and need the books week after week, these books can be kept on one side and brought out of 'reserve' when the class comes. This however, should be avoided if at all possible, because it restricts the number of books available for home reading. It will be appreciated that it would be unwise to arrange for classes to come to the library until it is stocked with an adequate supply of non-fiction books, particularly reference books, so that the children can use these without reducing unduly the supply of books for casual reading at home.

A less direct means of helping children is to prepare lists of recommended books. These can consist of recent additions to the library, of good books recommended for children of particular ages or on particular subjects of topical, or continuing general interest. They are useful whether it is possible to develop personal assistance with individual children or not, because they can be handed out to children, or children can help themselves to them and take them home. If class numbers are entered against the titles the children can use them as 'finding' lists for the books they want to read.

Such lists need not consist merely of authors and titles of books but may also include paragraphs about authors, about outstanding books, even about life in general providing books are quite definitely and specifically featured. The regular publication of a leaflet which comprises particulars of new books, information about the library service and other matters of general interest to children is useful and leads children directly to books. If possible, a children's list should be published separately from one for adults, and it is an advantage for it to be printed rather than duplicated. A printed leaflet looks better and is more attractive than a duplicated one; however, costs of production frequently determine the form such a publication should take. Let it not be overlooked, however, that the greater attractiveness and therefore the greater efficiency of the printed publication far outweighs the disadvantage of the extra cost.

To sum up, primarily a knowledge of children's books, and secondarily the ability to put this knowledge across to the children in a way which is attractive and acceptable to them are essential qualities in a children's librarian. Children's librarians, even the most senior ones who have a staff of assistants working under them in the children's library, find they need to be constantly handling books, getting to know the best books on certain subjects, keeping abreast of recent publications, and generally informing themselves of matters in which children are interested. The young children's librarian should not consider that the replacement of books on the shelves, or straightening shelves is a tedious, menial task. These duties, although they could be done by someone with less education and less well informed about books, constantly enlarge the assistant's knowledge of books and help her to prepare herself for the more responsible tasks which every worthwhile and enthusiastic children's librarian hopes one day to be able to perform. The children's librarian will read reviews of books printed in general and also literary periodicals as well as those which are intended specially for children; above all, she will read books which are written for children – before they are put on the library shelves if at all possible. In a large library it will be impossible for her to read them all; in this case she should read representative ones, and sample books by different authors, arranging for her colleagues to read other books. They would then discuss the books they had read. She would do this in order to get to know her stock, to know what kind of books are being written for children, and also to acquire knowledge and information which will help her to perform the important function of seeing that the right book goes to the right child when needed.

WORK WITH ADOLESCENTS

Children begin to borrow fewer books from public libraries at the age of twelve or thereabouts. This is partly due to the fact that they have to study very much more for public examinations, and to do more homework; they also spend more time on cultural pursuits such as learning to play a musical instrument, or on handicrafts. As they enter adolescence, they become very much more interested in group activities than previously, and develop an interest in members of the opposite sex. Their interests are very much wider, and they have very much more freedom, than previously; they tend to spend their free time out of their homes, and away from parental supervision. All these changes in their way of life tend to divert their attention from books. It is therefore essential for librarians, particularly public librarians, to try to stimulate and retain the interest of children as they reach the age of eleven so that they retain their connection with the library. One way of doing this is to invite them to become helpers in the library, working on a rota system at processing new books, repairing books, making scrap-books or cuttings books, putting returned books on the shelves, discharging books and issuing them to other members of the library, and helping the librarian in other ways. In many libraries, puppet groups, discussion groups, handicraft groups, play readings, film shows, talks and similar activities are organized to help keep the children in touch with the library. All these activities should be directed towards the use of books, and wherever possible a direct link should be made between these activities and the borrowing of books from the library.

When children reach the age of about thirteen they tend to feel they are becoming grown-up and consequently may want to use the adult library rather than the children's library. A large adult library can be overwhelming to a young person of this age.

While still members of the children's library, they should be allowed to enter the adult library to borrow any book they need which is not available in the children's library. On these occasions they should accompany a member of the staff who would help them find the book. In this way they will become familiar with the adult library and realize that it has something new to offer them at a time when they are growing out of the children's library.

The intermediate department

Many librarians have experimented with special provision for adolescents, mainly with the object of lessening the confusion which they are almost sure to feel when first entering an adult library, especially if it is a large one. One of the earliest experiments of this nature was to have a separate room containing books on all subjects which would be of interest to young people when they reached the age at which they were permitted to transfer from the children's library, and which they might use for a year or so before passing on to the adult library.

Rigidly kept age bars for transferring from the children's library to the intermediate library and then to the adult library are not satisfactory because there are very many children and adolescents who are quite capable of reading books intended for adults – and in fact are much more capable of reading and understanding them than many adults. Children may be allowed to use their children's library tickets in the intermediate or adult library until they are certain they wish to transfer, or until the normal time for renewal arrives.

The intermediate section
Probably the best, certainly the most economical, means of providing for adolescent boys and girls is to reserve a portion of the adult library for their use.

As there would be no special tickets or membership arrangements for using this section it might be necessary to discourage adult readers from depleting the carefully selected stock. Although it would be difficult to place a ban on their borrowing from these shelves, if it were pointed out that the books were intended for adolescents as an introduction to the adult library they would, generally speaking, respect the restriction.

The young people for whom this section is intended would not be restricted to the books there; they would, in fact, have the freedom of the whole adult library. They can be introduced to other sections of the library when they ask for books not in the intermediate section. The whole purpose of this section is to break down the feeling of awe which they experience when going into a huge library, and it is only intended to be used by these young people for a short period at the beginning of their membership of the adult library – only in fact until they feel they are sufficiently at home in the adult library to use the whole of the stock provided. If the design and shape of the lending library make it possible, these books should be kept in an alcove close to the entrance to the department and clearly labelled for adolescents so that the adult members of the library would feel that they were intruding if they went in there.

The book stock
The stock of books in the intermediate library, or section, would contain some books suitable for older boys and girls in the children's library and also some appropriate books in the adult library. It would include some of those generally considered to be children's classics (most of which, incidentally – except those written in the present century – were written originally for adults) and a generous, wisely chosen, selection of adult fiction. Novels, especially contemporary ones, would have to be chosen with great care to make sure that their moral tone was suitable. 'Cadet' editions (i.e. slightly shortened versions) of modern novels are especially acceptable. Such a collection would also include science fiction, westerns, adventure books, thrillers and some of the less lurid romances; the moral tone of such kinds of fiction is generally satisfactory. One needs also to look for books written in good English, for so many are trivial and poorly written. The non-fiction section would include books of an intermediate standard, and there should be a generous supply of books on civics, handicrafts, sport, science, travel, biography and other subjects which interest young people. Books on Christianity and other religions intended for adolescents (and there are many such on Christianity) should also find a place in this section of the library.

It is an excellent idea for these young people, when they reach the age at which they would normally be admitted to membership of the adult library, or when they are about to leave school, to be taken into the adult library and be shown round by a senior member of the staff. Although it would be emphasized that the intermediate library or section was mainly intended for them, and they were given every opportunity of examining the books there, it would be desirable to show them the whole of the adult stock and explain the arrangement of the books and of the catalogues. They would then feel at liberty either to use the intermediate collection or the adult library. Showing school leavers round as a regular part of co-operation with local schools is excellent publicity quite apart from its value to the individuals concerned.

Whenever a boy or girl is transferred at his request, or on the suggestion of the children's librarian, to the adult library, he should be taken by the children's librarian and personally introduced to a named senior member of the staff in the adult library; the adolescent should be mentioned by name, in his presence, as someone who is ready to use the adult library and who would like to have the library explained. This shows courtesy and friendliness to the member and helps to break down the barrier which so often exists between members of a library and the staff. This method of introduction is shown to bear fruit later when the new member encounters some difficulty and shows less than normal hesitation in going to the member of the staff to whom he was introduced, or even to another, and making his request. It is little courtesies like this which help to bring about good relations between staff and members, and a consequent improvement of the library service.

If there are youth clubs in the district, it is often helpful for the senior assistant concerned with the adolescent provision, to give talks to members on the library, its books, its activities, or even on some non-library subject. An invitation would be given to members of the club to visit the library, either in a body as an outing, or individually, in order to become acquainted with the facilities available.

The following section is concerned with extension activities which may be organized to attract children to the children's library. Similar extension activities can be organised in connection with the adult library, but with the intention of attracting adolescents to the library. Nothing is more encouraging than to see many young people in the upper forms of secondary schools, or who have just started work, using the library habitually. If a good book stock is provided, if relations with schools and youth clubs are good, and if activities are carried on at the library with the intention of attracting the interest of adolescents, there is every likelihood that the young people will make good use of the facilities provided.

EXTENSION WORK

Extension work is the name given to cover all kinds of activity carried out either inside or outside a library building to further the aims and objects of the library. Any activity which is concerned with people in groups, even informal groups, and is intended to result in greater use of the library, comes under this heading.

ACTIVITIES INSIDE THE LIBRARY

The organization of extension activities, and carrying them out, involves a considerable amount of time, and is normally undertaken only if staff can be spared from their work with books and readers. Moreover it must be remembered that these activities, however varied, will reach only a portion of the library's readers. It is therefore unwise to undertake this work unless the book stock is adequate and can meet any extra demands which the extension activities will make, for the librarian's *foremost* concern is to

provide a book stock of good quality which is large enough
to supply all his potential readers' needs.

Story hours

The oldest, and most often practised, of these activities
is the 'story hour' which has been an organized part of
children's libraries in America and England – as well as
other countries – for many years. Actually, each session
does not last an hour: half-an-hour is long enough; twenty
minutes is even better.

The purpose of story hours is primarily to interest children, particularly those under eight years of age, in good
stories and good literature. If story hours are popular they
can be held for children of different age groups: those under
six, six to eight, and nine and over. Story hours for the
oldest of these groups will be attended by fewer children than
the others, and one must expect children in the older groups
to bring with them younger brothers and sisters, for whose
activities they are temporarily responsible.

Stories must be chosen to suit the age group, bearing in
mind the smaller-than-intended who will be present;
fidgeting by small children whose attention has not been
captured can be very distracting to both other listeners and
story-teller. The stories should stimulate children to read
books, either those by the author whose story has been told,
or similar ones by other authors. Although they should be
complete in themselves they should not be told simply as
entertainment. If two or more stories are told in each 'hour',
each should be of a different type so as to provide a contrast.
Imaginative stories are preferable to realistic ones and they
should be told in such a way that the children's attention is
held the whole time.

The effective telling of stories requires great skill; some
people have a gift for it, and most can, by the reading of
books on the subject and with patient practice, acquire

considerable ability. Stories must under no circumstances be read, for much of the success of story-telling depends on the teller's being free to adapt his story to the audience as he goes along. Stories which are read aloud lose much of their charm unless the reading is done by someone with consummate skill and even then much of the effect is lost when the audience consists of children. The good story-teller reads the story over several times to herself to learn the gist of it (not to learn it word for word), and then rehearses it to herself either mentally or verbally (or better still, both) before telling it to the children. If she knows it thoroughly she can vary the actual telling (words and manner, shortening or expanding it) according to the reactions of her audience. The story must be told at one sitting and without breaks, interruptions or interference; any explanations which are needed, as they may be if the story's setting or subject matter is not likely to be within the understanding or experience of the audience, must be worked into the story so as to form a coherent part of it. Questions must not be asked as part of the telling, for some bright youngster is almost sure to give an immediate answer – and it may be one which will destroy the whole atmosphere or point of the story.

When? When should the story hours be given, and how often? These are matters which can only be determined in the light of local conditions. The best time is when children are likely to find it most convenient to attend, but often this is the time when staff can least be spared. A solution is to have storytellers from outside the staff. It is sometimes practicable, as the 'story hour' does not last very long, for it to be held an hour before a busy peak period, or when such a time begins to slacken. Once a week for each age group is often enough; fortnightly would be less satisfactory, for the children might have difficulty in remembering which was story hour week. Oftener would probably make too much demand on the story-tellers, specially if the staff were a small one, or there were only one or two able to tell stories effectively.

Where? Where should the stories be told? The best place is in the children's lending or reference library itself as it has the right atmosphere created by the books in the room. But this restricts the opportunities to times when the library is closed (for the library should be closed while stories are being told in order to prevent interruptions) – the very times when they would expect to draw least support. The best that one could do would be to hold story hours for the smallest children half-an-hour before the library was due to open in the afternoon – but what about the children who go to school, bearing in mind that the library is normally open when the schools are closed? And so 'time' affects 'place'. A children's lending or reference library should not normally be closed on any single day of the week (neither should an adult library for that matter), for a public library provides a public service and should be open every day during the same hours (whatever they may be) otherwise inconvenience is caused and people are prevented from making use of the service. Who amongst us has not seen people trying to enter a library on the one day of the week when it is closed? Children cannot be expected to remember which day the library is not open. But if the library *is* closed for a day or a half-day this is a more convenient day to hold the story hours.

If it is not possible for stories to be told in a room containing books, then a children's activities room, or a small spare room adjoining the children's room could be used. It should be adjacent to the junior library so that the children do not have to go through other departments. A room used for another purpose such as a store or an office should not be used because the furniture or other contents would create a distracting and unattractive atmosphere. It should be furnished with chairs of appropriate size and have a rug, carpet, or woven grass mat for the smallest children to sit on. Pictures which children can appreciate should be on the walls, and vases (of flowers if possible), models or toy animals should be on the window-sills to provide interest and atmosphere.

Some libraries provide a specially designed room with a carpeted raked floor and such extra features as windowless openings at which children or adults can appear at the appropriate moment during the dramatization of a story, and with special lighting effects. Rooms equipped in this way are not always suitable for use for other activities, and unless stories are told frequently, such rooms represent an uneconomic tying up of capital, and occupy space which could be used more frequently for various purposes in a more multi-purpose room.

Where it is not possible to provide a suitable room, or rooms, solely for the use of the children, then lecture halls or other rooms should be used.

In some libraries, especially American ones, story-telling areas are permanently arranged in the lending library. These consist of mediaeval type high back fireside seats, benches specially designed with curved seats holding four or six children and arranged in a circle, or some other form of permanent seating. There is usually a fire, either real or simulated wood log (which is currently fashionable in American branch libraries), or electric. An imitation log fire with a (too-regular) flickering glow, and heat, according to season, all produced by electricity is sometimes used to give 'atmosphere'. In my view this is all too formal. A story hour arrangement of furniture which is only in use at the most two hours a week but is *in situ* all the week – and unsuitably so – makes a fetish of a relatively unimportant aspect of the department's work. Moreover, such furniture is usually ugly, and valuable floor space is not used to the best advantage. If the room is to be used for story hours, it is better to use the ordinary furniture of the room, letting the children move it into position themselves, arranging it around a (real or imitation) fire if there is one.

In warm weather there is no reason why stories should not be told in the open air, except that the atmosphere of a library is lost. A shady position should be chosen, it should also be a quiet and secluded one to prevent the audience being distracted by passers-by, friends calling out, or disturbing traffic. Here, the children should sit on the ground unless there are tree-trunks arranged in scout or guide campfire fashion. Collapsible canvas chairs could be used, but formality should be avoided.

Picture book time
A variation of the story hour is picture book time. This caters for children who are generally too young to read but are able to appreciate picture books – normally most children between two and five. This form of library extension work can take place at almost any time and is specially suitable when the library is closed to children of school age. A particularly useful time is when parents visit the library to choose their own books and are pleased to be relieved of having to look after their children for twenty minutes or so. The children's librarian simply goes to the shelves, takes off suitable picture books, gathers three or four to a dozen children around her and reads the stories to the children, at the same time showing them the appropriate picture page.

Puppets
Puppet-making is popular as a handicraft and as a means of teaching speech training and developing self-expression. It can be used with story-telling, and is also a good form of entertainment. The children's librarian, in conjunction with the children, can decide on a well-known story from classical

49

or modern literature, or a historical incident; the children can meet weekly to make the puppets while others are learning to speak the story, and performances can subsequently be given to library members and their parents.

Plays

Play readings and even dramatic performances, particularly for an annual occasion such as a Christmas story festival or parents' day, are excellent ways of developing an interest in literature. So are 'new book evenings' at which new books are reviewed verbally and made available for borrowing, and book discussion groups at which children are encouraged to talk about, and read extracts from, books they have recently read. Both these activities, especially the latter, need considerable preparation and 'behind the scenes' encouragement by the children's librarian who will find she will get better results the more intimately she knows her members.

Stamp clubs

Stamp clubs at which members exchange stamps and hear a talk, illustrated by an appropriate display, about some aspect of stamp collecting, are always popular and bring many children to the library. A good collection of books for home reading, and also a variety in the junior reference library, should be provided to link the children's interests directly with their use of the library. In this way they get to realize the important part a library can play in their hobbies and non-academic, non-recreational interests.

All these activities require considerable organization, and often demand more time and effort than the staff of the department, even if there are three or four of them, can manage. The assistance of non-librarian friends who can be prevailed upon to take responsibility for organizing and running the various functions can make it possible for such activities to be carried on when they would otherwise have been impossible.

Film shows

Film shows are usually popular with children and well attended when they are held in the library (or out of doors in tropical climates), providing there is at least one humorous or other film of popular appeal in the 'programme'. The shows normally last about an hour and consist of short documentary or instructional films, especially made for children when available, with the humour or 'popular' item at the end. Feature films are not shown except at festival or commemoration times. At every showing something appropriate to the film programme is said about the library and its books, and a display of relevant books is arranged in the library.

Lectures and concerts

Lectures, or rather 'talks' for children, on a variety of subjects are given in many libraries. Concerts, or perhaps more appropriately, talks on music with musical illustrations, can also be usefully provided. These are most conveniently arranged in series, being held in the early evening, and last about forty-five minutes.

Lectures attract less support than was the case years ago. This is because so much attractive entertainment and instruction is available on television. They still perform a very useful function, however, where these competing attractions for children do not exist. If the librarian hopes to attract children to lectures it is necessary to hold them at times when children are less likely to be looking- or listening-in and to provide speakers as good as those engaged by the broadcasting authorities.

The following points should be borne in mind when planning for and 'running' talks: (a) avoid lecturers with speech impediments or mannerisms, or who 'speak down' to children; (b) use visual aids, demonstrations, or live musical illustrations whenever possible; (c) see that the preparation of the lecture room is complete long before the talk, and that all microphones, visual aids, emergency lights and doors, etc., are working properly; (d) arrange for the speaker to be at the hall half an hour before the talk is due to begin and see to it that he is informed of any organizational or administrative procedure, is willing to deal with any questions from the audience, etc. Before the talk he should have an opportunity for rest and relaxed conversation with a member of the staff in an effort to lessen any feeling of nervousness; (e) see that an adequate number of stewards are available in the hall to maintain discipline and ensure that the children leave the hall in an orderly manner.

Book weeks

One of the most rewarding methods of introducing children to books, and incidentally of introducing children and sometimes their teachers, to the library, is to organize book weeks. These consist of two or three talks each morning and afternoon, the children being brought in classes by their teachers from the local schools. Talks are given by authors and illustrators of children's books, by publishers, booksellers or librarians, or by musicians, sportsmen or explorers, all with a view to drawing attention to books and the part they play in the life of the child.

They are supplemented by an attractively displayed and colourful exhibition of books from the library or on loan from booksellers or publishers, the books remaining on view throughout the period of the lectures and perhaps two or three days afterwards. Visitors must be able to handle the books.

The extensiveness of these book weeks, the type of speakers who take part, and the exact form the weeks take depend on the situation of the library in relationship to the availability of speakers and the ease with which books can be obtained for display. In large British and American towns it is obviously much easier than in more remote places; in some overseas countries it is very difficult, and such attempts at this kind of activity must depend on likely speakers visiting the town for other purposes, or 'passing through'.

These weeks require much preparation months in advance, discussing with teachers the form the week is to take, arranging speakers, borrowing books and display fittings, arranging for the attendance of children in school time, the printing of tickets of admission, programmes and booklists, and hiring films if these are to be included in the programme.

Adequate funds must be available, for all these items cost money, and all the speakers should be paid a fee and also their expenses.

ACCOMMODATION FOR MAJOR ACTIVITIES

Lectures, concerts, film shows and similar activities need a hall which will hold between 100 and 200 children. Local building and fire regulations will specify such matters as the fastening of chairs in rows, gangways, the number and position of exits, staircases, fittings for emergency exit doors, emergency lighting for exit signs, etc. These are very important matters in connexion with halls which are to be used by children, and the regulations must be complied with. Plays are always popular; if these are to be performed it is necessary to have a hall with a suitable stage, special lighting, 'green rooms' and toilets behind the stage, and enough space to keep props and scenery when not in use.

THE ACTIVITIES ROOM AND ITS EQUIPMENT

A children's Activities Room situated as part of the Work with Young People suite of rooms, can be used for all the activities undertaken in the library which do not comprise the issue of books for home reading and reference, providing attendances are limited to about thirty, and catering for children of pre-school age to about fourteen years. Such a room needs more equipment than if it were used for one purpose only by children of one age group. Tables, low and small but rigid, and some collapsible ones, as well as enough chairs of two or three sizes, each to half-fill the room at least, will be required. Cupboards with lockable sliding doors for equipment and apparatus, and shelves for exhibiting models, sculpture and other objects will be needed; provision should also be made for displaying pictures permanently and temporarily, and for pinning up drawings. Projectors for showing-colour transparencies of two sizes (35 mm. and $2\frac{1}{4}''$ x $2\frac{1}{4}''$) and films are essential. A portable screen is suitable for a small room, but a roll screen permanently fixed to the ceiling, which can be unrolled for use by releasing cords is most suitable in a large room: this should be fitted behind a beam, false wall, cornice or pelmet so as to obscure it when not in use. A wall painted with flat white water paint makes a good screen providing the wall is flat. A white screen area surrounded by another colour tends to look unsightly when not actively in use but can be easily and attractively concealed with floor to ceiling curtaining.

The walls can have peg-board (hard-board with holes bored into it at about $\frac{1}{2}''$ intervals all over its surface) fixed to them for display of objects or books. Brackets and hooks of various kinds and sizes can be purchased for fitting into the holes to display objects, but as they can be easily knocked off, fragile objects should be placed on a shelf or cupboard top.

Drawing-pins cannot be put into hard-board, and some other means must be found for displaying drawings, book-jackets, unframed pictures, etc. The most suitable background material to use is cork consisting of small grains of cork pressed into sheets. Although by the nature of the cork it closes up on the withdrawal of pins, after a considerable time drawing-pin holes will appear to pit the surface, so the finest possible pins should be used. Cork does not need decorating and is best left in its natural state. The various forms of soft-board are less satisfactory in that the surface wears away more quickly and more extensively, and it must be painted from time to time. Drawing-pin holes are much more conspicuous in it. The walls could have different surfaces affixed to them so as to permit different methods of display; alternatively, screens (which should be collapsible but rigid when assembled) could be used. Screens should be constructed so that three or more can be interlocked; this avoids the necessity of having to provide feet to support them. People always seem to trip over such feet. The bottom of the display area should be 1 foot 9 inches, and the top 5 feet, from the floor.

Framed pictures look best if no cords suspending them from a picture-hook on a picture-rail are visible. To make this possible, aluminium alloy rails with a slot running along them are fixed at suitable heights, say 3 feet and 5 feet from the floor. If the pictures have short screws with large heads screwed into the back of the upright sides of the frames with the head and one eighth of an inch of the shank of the screw projecting, the screwheads can be inserted in an opened portion of the slot in the aluminium strip and slid along the rail to the desired hanging position. This keeps them securely in position and helps to reduce the possibility of theft. The rails should be fixed flush with the wall, and peg-board or cork can be fixed below them.

As it is desirable to have the bottom of the pictures level the screws must be fixed exactly at a pre-determined distance from the bottom of the picture-frames.

A furniture store-room should be provided adjoining the Activities Room so that furniture which is not wanted for any particular function can be stored out of sight.

Rail in section screwed
to batten which is
fastened to wall.

Picture-frame showing screw
in position in rail.

Rail showing cut-out position to
allow for insertion of screws in back
of frame.

Records of activities

Complete records (date, function, title of story, talk or film, etc., attendance) of all these activities should be kept in a departmental diary, as a permanent record, and details should be included on the weekly report forms (and in brief form on the monthly and quarterly report forms) sent to the Chief Librarian.

ACTIVITIES OUTSIDE THE LIBRARY

There are other activities which can be undertaken outside the library with the purpose of expanding the libraries' service to the public, and which can therefore correctly be said to be included in an extension programme.

Bulk loans

One such activity is the sending of collections of books to schools, youth clubs, homes for orphans, or to children who have to be housed temporarily away from their own homes in hospitals, remand homes, borstals, or schools for handicapped children. It will be seen that two kinds of groups are mentioned here: (a) those whose members are limited in their movements, who may even be restricted to using one building and having no freedom or ability to move from it, and (b) those who are not so confined. The type of service provided for the latter might be considered more in the nature of a propaganda service, it being hoped that the children would want to go to a library to borrow their books. This is always desirable, for the habit of using a library is one which every child should develop. Bulk loans should not normally be sent to places where the occupants could easily go to a public library, and would only be made when the nearest static library or mobile library 'station' was too far away for the children to use it.

No form of book provision is so beneficial to the user from the points of view of (a) providing him with what he needs and (b) giving the 'feel' and 'atmosphere' of a library, as a library room providing a full lending and reference service. This form of provision can be made within limits by large bulk loans. It is an advantage if books sent in bulk always comprise a number of units, each of say 25 or 50 volumes. Both the library staff and those who receive the books then always know exactly how many books are on loan. The selection of books would be chosen to meet the particular needs of the children concerned, however unusual these might be; in any case they would have to be of the appropriate age range.

Should there be several centres or institutions to which books are to be sent it would be desirable to have specially made boxes for despatching the books, and to have a uniform system for dealing with the loans. The boxes could be made in such a way that the lid, when open, could serve as a shelf for displaying the books: each box would then have the equivalent of two short shelves, the base of the box serving as the second shelf. The boxes should not be too large and should be made of plywood on a framework made of light-weight wood, or aluminium alloy, and should have the equivalent of a hasp and staple so that they could be pad-locked to prevent pilfering when not in use. If they are made as indicated and have a handle at one end they can be carried by one person.

Each book should have two book-cards, one which is retained in the library when a book is sent as part of a bulk loan, and one which goes with the book and serves as a loan record card. They may both be the same size for convenience, but of a different colour so that there can be no mistake when making up a batch. Author, title, class number and accession number would be written at the top of each card. The loan record card would need three columns for the insertion of the date of lending, the reader's name, and the date of return. These details would be written in by the person appointed to be honorary librarian. The other card would be the head-quarters loan card and have recorded on it the date of loan and the loan box number or the name of the centre to which it was sent. If loan box numbers were used, a separate record of the date, and centre to which the boxes were sent, would have to be kept. Were the details mentioned not needed on the individual cards they could be kept behind a guide or another card, bearing the name or number of the centre, the box number and the date of loan.

Such bulk loans gradually become organized as the service develops, into a regular system or even department, perhaps requiring a separate stock and possibly separate staff to deal with the work involved. 'Book box' systems and 'school libraries' as provided by public libraries, are of this nature; the books are collected just before the end of each school term, and are looked through during the holidays to deter-mine which copies need re-binding, repair or replacing.

The books in the respective boxes are made up to the proper numbers, the name of the school entered on the cards which are assembled in batches, secured with elastic bands, dated with the date of despatch, and the book-cards for the entering of loan records placed in the boxes after checking for accuracy. The boxes are sent to the schools on the first day of the next term.

The routines for dealing with bulk loans to other centres may be the same as to schools except that exchanges may be made at any time.

Talks on the work of the library

One of the most effective extension activities that the children's librarian can perform is visiting schools, youth clubs, children's hospitals and homes, to give talks on the library and on the books in it, at the same time displaying copies of colourful, attractive book-jackets. She would on these occasions leave for distribution copies of library bulletins, lists of new books, special book lists and programmes of forthcoming story hours, talks, film shows, etc. If she were a competent story-teller, she could give a story hour as an advertisement for those held at the library. If the library had a puppetry team they could give a performance. Co-operation of this kind, if it can be developed, is extremely valuable for the success of the library.

CHAPTER II

Books and their Use

BOOK SELECTION

Aims

A library without a good selection of books is a misnomer, and one of the most important functions of a children's librarian is to see that an adequate number of the best books available is put into stock.

The aims of the children's library should be to see that children's needs for books of (a) information and (b) recreation are fully met. They should be provided with books which will enable them to increase their knowledge and understanding of themselves, of the people they see about them and of the world they live in. It is essential therefore to provide a wide selection of story books, and of non-fiction books for reference and also for home reading. Children's library work will fail unless adequate numbers of the best of all kinds of books are provided, and unless the children *enjoy* reading them. The books must therefore be suitable for the children's age and reading development so that they may find books that not only interest them, but actually fascinate them.

Principles of book selection

It is important to ensure that the numbers of books in all non-fiction subjects are properly balanced. There must be enough books of all degrees of difficulty to meet the needs of the young readers on all subjects they are likely to want to read about. There must also be a larger number of books (and this may mean duplicating titles) on subjects which are popular. Bias in book selection should be avoided. It would be foolish, for example, to provide a large number of books written from say a Protestant point of view in a district where the majority of people were Roman Catholics and to provide very few books on Roman Catholicism. Both points of view must be adequately and fairly represented, and in such a case as this it would not be unreasonable if there were a larger number of books written from the Roman Catholic point of view. This is normal practice in book provision and applies to all subjects, but particularly to religious, political and international subjects.

It is also important to see that the book fund is fairly distributed between non-fiction books and story books: the bulk of the money should not be spent on story books just because these are in greater demand than non-fiction titles. If one wishes to encourage the reading of non-fiction one must provide an adequate quantity of such books. Owing to the rapid development of libraries for children in recent years a wide selection of books on non-fiction subjects is now available, even for quite small children. Details of non-fiction books may have to be sought from bibliographical sources such as those mentioned later; one cannot rely only on local bookshops for one's purchases (although many shops which sell books have a selection of children's books), or from lists prepared by booksellers or publishers, because these do not represent or indicate the total number or even a wide selection of the non-fiction books which are available. Most of the booksellers who specialize in supplying public libraries carry a very large stock of suitable books and also circulate stock lists. These are very helpful.

In order to avoid an unbalanced stock, it is necessary to ensure that a large collection of books is not provided for one group of readers at the expense of another; for example, many school stories for girls and very little science fiction. One must try and meet the *demands* of readers and at the same time supply books to meet other needs. Children's reading should not be confined to one kind of book or one kind of story. They may get tired of one kind, and if there is not a wide choice they will cease to use the library because they cannot find anything else which attracts them. Children grow out of a particular kind of book or of desiring books by a particular author; a wide selection of books makes it possible for them to experiment in their reading and to read as widely as possible. If children do not develop the habit of selective and varied reading there is every chance that when they grow into adulthood their reading will continue to be along very narrow and unadventurous lines.

There are many varieties of books in the English language, not only as regards content but also as regards make-up. This is also true of books in most European languages, but the number of books in some of the Asian and African languages, especially for children, is very limited. In these cases reliance must continue to be made on European books or on European books which have had translations into the local languages written by hand on the printed pages (this is only possible in the case of books for younger readers where there is little text interspersed with the illustrations), until literacy in the local languages has developed to such a degree as to make publication a commercial proposition or where publication is made possible by government subsidies.

The books chosen for a children's library should be representative of the best style of writing that exists. Books which are not well written should not be bought. Books which are recognized by librarians, educators and writers as being 'standard', and good literary texts, should be available in fairly large quantities. Books which the children's librarian considers especially good and which she would like the children to read because of their good quality, should be duplicated to such an extent that at least one copy (but not too many because this might give the children the impression that the books were not being read and therefore not popular) is always on the shelves. This gives the children's librarian opportunities of encouraging the children to read good books, for when they go to her and ask for recommendations, or when in the course of conversation with them she has opportunities of recommending good books, she can wander around the shelves with the children and always be sure of finding something suitable. It should always be possible to find something worth recommending on the shelves. The acknowledged masterpieces of the children's literature of the country, and of other countries, should always be available to offer to children.

In building up the initial stock of the library, in buying new books, and in occasional improvement of the stock class by class, it is desirable to keep constantly in mind the need for a proper balance of books of good quality. There are several useful guides to the choice of books for a children's library. Unfortunately, publishers do not always keep good books in print, and therefore one must constantly refer to recently published lists of books compiled by responsible individuals, or groups of persons recognized as having a good knowledge of children's literature. The following are recommended:

Crouch, Marcus, *editor. Books about children's literature: a booklist prepared by the Committee of the Youth Libraries Group.* Rev. ed. Library Association. 1966.

Lewis, Naomi. *The best children's books of 1967.* Hamish Hamilton, 1968.
> A handy selected record of books published during one year. All entries have annotations, some quite lengthy. Volumes for 1963, 1964 and 1965 were also published.

Library Association. *Books for young people, Group I: Under eleven.* 2nd. ed. 1960.
> Has two 'bridges' for ages 9-11 and 14-16 year olds.

Library Association. *Books for young people, Group II: Eleven to thirteen plus.* Compiled by the North Midland Branch 3rd rev. ed. 1960.

Library Association. *Books for young people, Group III: Fourteen to seventeen.* 1957.

Lines, Kathleen. *Four to fourteen.* 2nd ed. National Book League. 1956.

> The major list of current children's books containing 2,000 items with annotations.

National Book League. *Additions to your school library.*

> The second supplement to the dispersed School Library Exhibition of 1960. The books listed were published between June 1962 and December 1963 and are suitable for children between 5 and 15. No annotations.

National Book League. *British children's books.* 3rd ed. 1967.

> Contains representative titles by British authors, arranged in four chronological groups, the last (1961-67) being divided into fiction and non-fiction. All entries are annotated.

National Book League. *School library books: non-fiction.* 2nd. ed. 1968.

> Catalogue of books included in an exhibition. A guide for buying a basic stock. All entries are annotated.

School Library Association. *Eleven to fifteen: a basic list of non-fiction for secondary school libraries.* Compiled by Peggy Heeks. 3rd. ed. 1963.

> 1000 books arranged by fairly broad subject groups with author and subject indexes and annotations as necessary.

School Library Association. *Books for primary children.* Edited by Berna Clark. 3rd ed. of *Primary school library books.* 1968.

Shor, Rachel and Fidell, Estelle A, *editors. Children's catalog: a class catalog of 4274 children's books recommended for public and school libraries, with an author, title and subject index.* 11th ed. New York, H. W. Wilson, 1966.

> Four annual supplements will cover approximately 1200 additional titles.

Basic stock

The number of books for a basic stock cannot be predetermined but a large children's library should contain about 2,000 different *titles* (not *copies*), a third being non-fiction and two-thirds fiction, all specially chosen for their good quality. If a large number of young children live in the

64

district, there should be a wide choice of books for 'tiny tots' so that they can develop the habit of reading books at an early age. The age group for which most provision will need to be made is the 8–11 group, as it is from children of these ages that most of the members will come.

In addition to lending library books, up to about 900 reference books are also needed, the number depending on the size of the library. These would include primarily dictionaries, gazetteers, atlases, literary texts of various kinds, annuals giving all kinds of information about different countries and about the world as a whole, encyclopaedias, biographical dictionaries, year books, etc.

Details of books of this kind can be found in the School Library Association's *List of books on librarianship and library technique, and general reference books.* Some reference books are also mentioned in the Library Association's *Books for young people.* The number and subject range of the stock of books in the reference library will depend very largely on the type of district in which the library is situated and the need for books of this nature. In a library which is surrounded by schools or is visited by fairly large numbers of older children, and also in a country where homework and individual private study are encouraged by school teachers, it is desirable to have a fairly large collection of reference books especially where school libraries are non-existent or inadequate. Where co-operation with local schools extends to children coming to the library in class time to undertake private study or project work it is absolutely essential to have a fairly large and varied collection of reference books of all kinds and also to have them in duplicate so that several copies can be used simultaneously by children following the same or related subjects. The definition of the word 'reference' will also need to be much more all-embracing in this case than the usual definition which confines the meaning to books in which the contents are presented in such a way that one would not wish, or be able, to read the book right through. The stock will need to include reliable books in which the facts are presented succinctly and clearly. Good indexes are essential in such books. Children who are undertaking project work and only come to the school once a week for about three-quarters of an hour need to have the same books on each visit. Such books may be kept in the reference section, otherwise they may not be available on a subsequent visit and work cannot therefore be continued.

Responsibility for book selection
In small public libraries the selection of books for the children's library is done by the librarian, but in the larger library systems where there is a fairly large staff and where there is a separate children's department (which should be the criterion for deciding this matter), there should be an assistant specially trained and experienced in children's library work who should be entirely responsible to the librarian for the running of the whole of the children's library service as a separate department. This assistant should have full responsibility for deciding what books and periodicals should be added to stock subject to general directions and oversight from the librarian. Children's books form a special and separate field of literature, and the chief librarian cannot be expected to have (although he may quite well do so) a specialist knowledge of this branch of literature as well as of books for adults.

Choosing recent publications
However good the basic stock is, the library cannot maintain its efficiency, or its appeal to its users, unless the basic stock is extended by constantly adding new books as they are published. In fact the continuing success of any library depends very largely on the addition of new and good books in adequate quantities to meet the demands of its readers.

Particulars of such books can be obtained by going to book shops, by discussing children's books with other librarians and school teachers, by glancing through publishers' catalogues, by reading periodicals to see what is being currently written for children, and by consulting reviews of books published in periodicals.

Too much reliance should not be placed on particulars of books which appear in publishers' catalogues, as the comments are obviously prepared with the sole purpose of selling books and are not critical or disinterested. Publishers' catalogues are useful as guides.

The National Book League issues lists of books on specific subjects from time to time. The County Libraries Section of the Library Association also issues lists of books on specific subjects. These are much longer and are printed. The lists prepared by these organizations are seldom of books specifically for children but the lists can be used with great advantage by the librarians in charge of libraries for older children.

Useful guides to the selection of current literature are: the *British National Bibliography* (weekly with quarterly and annual cumulations) contains bibliographical particulars (but no annotations except to indicate which are children's books) of books published in Great Britain and deposited at the Copyright Office of the British Museum. All the books are classified by 'Dewey'. Similar publications are issued in Australia, the *Australian National Bibliography*, in India, the *Indian National Bibliography*, and in South Africa, the *South African National Bibliography*. *The School Librarian and School Library Review*, published three times a year by the School Library Association, contains annotated lists of new books and also annotated lists of books on special subjects. *Junior Bookshelf*, published quarterly, contains excellent reviews of recent publications, written by school and children's librarians. The *Children's Book News* is a bi-weekly review of new books chosen by the review panel consisting of children's librarians, parents and teachers, which has been appointed by the Children's Book Centre, a London bookshop. *Growing Point*, published ten times a year, contains reviews of more children's books than any other publication. *The Teacher*, published weekly, is recommended for its book reviews. *The Times Educational Supplement*, published weekly, always has about three pages of reviews of books varying from simple books for school children to books for adults. *The Times Literary Supplement* publishes twice a year a special children's number, and frequently includes children's books in the weekly issues. This is extremely useful in selecting contemporary books although the book reviews are not, generally speaking, very evaluative. From this point of view *The Times Educational Supplement* is a much more useful guide. The *Guardian* publishes a children's book supplement four times a year, and a number of literary weeklies review children's books twice a year; of these, *The Listener* is particularly useful. The work of children's librarians in obtaining bibliographical particulars of recently published books will be greatly simplified after *Children's books in print* commences publication in 1969. Reviews of books recommended in the Children's Books Section of *The booklist and subscription books bulletin*, the semi-monthly reviewing periodical of the American Library Association, were published by the A.L.A. in collected form in 1966 and 1967 under the title *Books for Children*.

Periodicals. It is advisable to have in every children's library a small selection of periodicals which are specially published for children. There are not many of these, but the following can be safely recommended: *Animals, Finding Out, Look and Learn, New Knowledge.* Periodicals are well worth providing because they (a) contain short articles on recent events and discoveries, thus supplementing books; (b) provide attractively information which children would probably overlook; (c) attract children to the library and encourage them to read in it rather than to use it merely as a place from which to borrow books. They are best displayed in specially designed shelving or stands so that the front covers are visible, and new issues should be put on display as soon as they are received from the supplier. There is no reason why comics should not be available in a children's library providing their standard of writing and of content conform to the principles already mentioned. Children enjoy reading comics, and their interest in humour is thereby developed. Humour can be conveyed very much more quickly and more subtly by drawings than by words, and this is the chief value of comics except for children whose reading ability is substandard. Comics, or stories which are simply written and illustrated by drawings, have a very useful function in developing children's reading ability, and are valuable in this connection. Comics however should be chosen with great care for some of them are quite unsuitable for children, and instead of developing those aspects of character which were mentioned earlier as being desirable they encourage those which are not. One of the chief responsibilities of the children's librarian is to see that unsuitable reading matter, whether books or periodicals, is not placed in the library.

Some of the adult periodicals are quite suitable for use in the children's library, e.g. the *Illustrated London News*, *Amateur Photographer*, *Argosy*, *Punch*, *The National Geographic Magazine*, *Geographical Magazine*, *Pictorial Education*.

The illustrations collection
Many librarians maintain an illustrations collection, although not very many of them allow the illustrations so provided to be used by children. A collection of illustrations of all kinds and on all subjects, cut from various sources and mounted on standard size mounts of $14\frac{1}{2}''$ x $10''$ is an extremely useful adjunct to a children's library. In many libraries the use of such illustrations is restricted to adult

teachers, artists and business men who need reliable information of various kinds in connection with their work, but
experience at Mitcham has shown that children can use
illustrations of this kind to great advantage, in connection
with their hobbies and their school work, in broadening
their knowledge of various aspects of life and of the world.
Illustrations are mostly obtained from superseded periodicals
which are marked up by the children's librarian, and cut
up and mounted by children who act as library helpers.
Worn out books, industrial house journals and travel publicity are also excellent sources of material. Every illustration
should be classified by Dewey (or in a large collection by
U.D.C.) just as are the books on the shelves, and a subject
index compiled giving entries under alternative headings (not
cross-references as these are time wasting and annoying to
the user) as generously as possible.

As an alternative to classifying, which requires the skill
of a classifier, a form of co-ordinate indexing may be used.
This work can be carried out by a clerk. All the illustrations
are given a consecutive number on being added to the
collection, and they are arranged in this order. No illustration of a particular object can be found without first consulting the index, but as the indexing is done thoroughly and
in respect of every important object included in the illustration, this method enables the utmost value to be obtained
from the collection. Take as an example a photograph of a
church. This may include a lych gate, a Gothic porch and a
Norman tower surmounted by a weathervane of such unusual
design as to justify indexing. A card with a subject heading
for each of these items (and any others which the photograph
justified) would be made out and the number of the particular
illustration entered on each. In order to simplify searching
for numbers, they are entered in columns according to the
last figure. This method, because it enables any one of a
number of items to be recorded, is more effective than

normal classifying (unless the U.D.C. were used – and this requires to be carried out by an expert), for this would, in the example quoted, enable a person to find only an illustration of a church without very detailed subject indexing; unless this were done, none of the other items could be discovered except by examining carefully all the illustrations of churches, and if it was the detail of the weathervane that was needed one would have to look at photographs of all kinds of buildings which might, or might not, have a weathervane. An added advantage of this form of co-ordinate indexing is that one's search can be narrowed down considerably. Supposing one wanted weathervanes containing sailing ships, but erected only on coach-houses, one would look at cards for weathervanes, ships and coach-houses and compare the numbers on each; the same numbers which appeared on *all three* cards would indicate the illustrations known to give the exact information required. The following are three cards from such a file:

CHURCHES

0	1	2	3	4	5	6	7	8	9
10	21	22	13	34	45	16	87	98	79
30	51	62	73	124	105	216	187	198	199
90	61	72	83	134	205	316	217	398	409
120	71	82	93	154	295	376	407	408	729

GERMANY

0	1	2	3	4	5	6	7	8	9
20	31	42	13	34	25	36	77	118	89
40	41	82	73	124	95	316	147	218	149
110	61	132	93	164	105	526	217	328	219

TOWERS, Buildings with

0	1	2	3	4	5	6	7	8	9
20	21	32	63	44	45	26	77	88	69
50	61	162	113	64	85	116	97	108	129
80	81	172	123	124	105	126	117	128	139

The headings, or subjects, are called 'keywords' or 'des-scriptors' in information retrieval terminology. The cards are called 'uniterm' or 'feature' cards and on them are recorded the numbers of all illustrations which depict churches, or an object or view in Germany, or buildings with towers. It will be noticed that the entries are listed by the last digit. If one wanted illustrations of German churches with a tower, one would look for numbers which appeared on each of the cards: 61, 124 and 105 are such. Numbers 20 and 77 are of buildings (other than churches) in Germany which have towers; numbers 21 and 45 are of churches with towers, and numbers 82, 13, 73, 93, 34, 316 and 217 are of churches in Germany which do not have towers.

It takes time searching the columns for identical numbers, but this is a simple system which a clerk can operate and has the advantage of not requiring expensive equipment. From the point of view of speed in finding simple illustrations, however, classification has an advantage over co-ordinate indexing. If a child wants illustrations of churches, they will all be found at one classification number, but with co-ordinate indexing the index cards will indicate the numbers of the appropriate illustrations, and each will have to be taken from the numbered sequence. This is a much more tedious method. Returning the illustrations to their sequence is equally tedious.

The illustrations are issued in cloth-covered cardboard portfolios such as are used by artists and collectors for keeping water colours and prints. The size of the front and back boards are 1″ larger than the largest mount and the joint joining the two boards is about ¾″ wide. Attached to the back board are flaps at top, bottom and side which turn in on top of the mounted illustrations when placed on the inside of the open back board. Tapes fastened to the outer edges of the long sides of both boards are tied and so secure the mounts in position for carrying.

CLASSIFICATION

Books can be placed on the shelves of a library (a) in no order at all, (b) roughly according to main subject, or (c) in classified order. Method (a) is satisfactory in one's personal library or in a very small children's library where the librarian is familiar with the position of individual books; (b) is adequate for a small collection or where 'fixed location' is supplemented by satisfactory catalogues; (c) is the only satisfactory method, even if the number of non-fiction books will not be more than 500 or so. The stock will grow over the years, and as it grows so the difficulties of finding individual books will become greater. When children ask for particular books, or for books on non-fiction subjects, one wants to be able to take them (sometimes after the ritual – carried out especially to instruct them without their being aware of it – of consulting the index to the classification, and perhaps the catalogue) to the shelves where the books should be. The use of a children's library is an excellent introduction to the mysteries and apparent confusions which people often experience when first using an adult library. If children are familiar with a well-administered children's library they will already be trained for using the adult library.

The need for orderly arrangement

In any walk of life where there are a number of objects, each of which appears to be somewhat similar but is really very different, and any particular one of which may be required at a moment's notice, it is necessary to have a well-defined – and well-kept – systematic order. The books in a children's library are no exception. This is one of three reasons for the orderly arrangement of books – to be able to find particular books easily and quickly. The others are: to have together all the books on the *same* subject, and to have together groups of books on *related* subjects.

Classifying books is placing together, in appropriate 'classes' according to a scheme of classification, those books which have certain common characteristics, and separating them from those which have other characteristics. This classifying process subsequently involves marking the books on the back of the title-page and on the spine, with the class number. This number is also put, not necessarily at the same time or by the same person, on the catalogue cards and any other records where the class number of the book is required, for it is the symbol indicating where the book will be found on the shelves, and also where a record of it will be found in the classified catalogue. The class number consists of the appropriate notation according to the scheme of classification in use, and often has, in addition, in a library of several thousand books, the first three letters of the author's surname; it is then known as a 'call number'. This enables the books to be arranged easily in alphabetical order within their classes, and so found quickly.

Arranging books in this systematic way enables the children to find easily specific books or books and information on a given topic – and this is what they usually require. The librarian is not always available for consultation, and an adequate catalogue of books arranged according to the scheme of book classification enables the children to be more independent of the librarian for their straightforward and ordinary needs.

Most libraries for children grow into quite considerable collections, and it is very important that there should be no chaos on the book-shelves at any time. Classification is therefore necessary, and it is desirable to choose a recognized scheme which successive librarians understand and can operate, for this may avoid the re-classifying of books in the future – a troublesome and time-consuming operation.

Books which are arranged in classified order suggest the whole range of human knowledge and experience (or in a children's library as much of it as is within the children's comprehension) and the interrelation of its parts in a way that no disorderly or ill-arranged collection can do.

A librarian can also observe any weakness or gaps in the stock which an unclassified library will not reveal.

Classification schedules are compiled by those who have lived for many years with the problems and requirements of libraries and their users, and who have consequently evolved sequences of subject arrangements on a scientific and logical basis. Knowledge is divided into main classes; these are divided into divisions which are in turn divided and sub-divided until the smallest item of knowledge is arrived at.

A good scheme of book classification should:

(1) be comprehensive, covering the whole field of know-ledge

(2) be logical in construction, and reproduce as far as possible the natural relationships of subjects

(3) provide places for the smallest and most specific item of knowledge and have facilities for the extension of the schedules to accommodate newly discovered knowledge

(4) have a simple and easily understood yet extensible notation

(5) have an adequate index

Home-made schemes

Persons who are not trained librarians sometimes think that they can devise a workable scheme, or that a known scheme is not suitable for their particular needs.

A satisfactory general scheme for the classification of books depends on the compiler having a comprehensive awareness of the whole of knowledge, a logical mind, the ability to compile and sub-divide schedules and index them so that they can be used by any librarian, and also the competence to devise an adequate notation. This demands much of any individual, and the general opinion of those who have closely examined or used home-made schemes is that these are not as satisfactory as the published and widely-used schemes, and that home-made schemes are certainly not worth the time and thought that has to be devoted to their compilation. Such schemes may be satisfactory when they are first compiled and the number of books is small, but they may break down as the collection increases in size. The sub-division of parts of the schedules may be difficult or even impossible when it is necessary to accommodate new knowledge or overlooked items. A subsequent librarian may consider that the schedules or the notation, or both, of a home-made scheme are illogical or otherwise unsatisfactory, and may wish to reclassify the books by another scheme. Even schemes drawn up by experts and compiled after a lifetime of experience and study are open to criticism.

The choice of a scheme
Method (c) on page 74, i.e. arranging the books in classified order is the situation in mind in this chapter. In order to meet the requirements mentioned, one of the several general schemes of systematic classification is normally used. The Dewey Decimal Classification is used more than any other in children's libraries, and indeed in public libraries throughout the English-speaking world, and this is the most important argument that can be used in its favour. There are others, such as: (a) the permanent organization based on the Library of Congress which provides for the continuous revision of the schedules; (b) the many book lists and bibliographies which are arranged in 'Dewey order' and give Dewey class numbers against the entries; of such is the *British National Bibliography* which has listed all British books published since 1952 (no other scheme is used so extensively in this way); (c) the ease with which it may be adapted and amended according to local needs.

There are other schemes of classification which it is

possible to use, such as Bliss's Bibliographic Classification,[1] and the Cheltenham Classification[2] designed for use in the Cheltenham Ladies' College, but neither of these has any outstanding merit for use in a small library, especially in a developing country, or in a children's or school library compared with the Dewey Classification.

CATALOGUING

It is desirable to have a list of all the books in the children's library in order to be able to say definitely whether or not a particular book is in stock, to direct a reader to the place on the shelves where it will be found, or to reserve it. Whether, in these days of costly materials and high salaries, the provision of a catalogue is justified is open to question. In some libraries facsimile teleprinting devices or Telex teleprinters have been installed to save the cost of providing catalogues at branches. Ideally there should be a catalogue so that members may be able to make full and purposeful use of the library. Members expect to know what is in stock, and if they are to be encouraged to use the library seriously they should be able to find out for themselves what the library's holdings are. If there were no catalogue they would have to ask the children's librarian to consult her list of books, and this they might do when she was busy and hardly able to spare time to deal with them. Being able to use a catalogue is also good preparation for using the adult library. Some sort of working list of books in stock must be available for the

---

[1] Bliss, H.E., *A Bibliographic Classification* . . . 4 vols. 1940-53
Bliss Classification Working Party. *The abridged Bliss Classification; the Bibliographic Classification of Henry Evelyn Bliss revised for school libraries.* School Library Association. 1967.

[2] Fegan, E.S., *and* Cant, M., *The Cheltenham Classification: a library classification for schools.* 2nd ed. 1958

children's librarian, and in these days of mechanical repro-
duction of catalogue entries, the production of a set of
entries is so much simpler than it was when every one had to
be separately typed, that the preparation of a public catalogue can be done at the same time as the librarian's list –
providing the latter is on separate slips.

What kind of catalogue?
The catalogue should be of the same kind and compiled
similarly to the one in the adult library so that (a) the
children have no difficulty in understanding the adult catalogue when they transfer to the adult library, (b) the work of
the staff is simplified by having only one kind of catalogue
to make, (c) many of the entries can be identical and serve
for both adult and children's library catalogues; this last is
a great advantage in a small library.

A reader can find the answer to the following questions by
consulting the catalogue: (a) what books by a particular
author are there in the library? (b) what books are there on
a particular subject? (c) what books are published in a particular series? (d) is a book with a particular title in the
library? Author entries will answer question (a), subject
entries (b), series entries (c), and title entries (d).

Dictionary or classified?
Catalogues are usually of two kinds, 'dictionary' and 'classified'. A book catalogued in a dictionary catalogue would
have a main entry which is the author entry, one or more
subject entries, entries (which may be 'added' entries – i.e.
similar to the main entry as far as fullness goes – or references to the main entry) under editors' or illustrators'
names, entries for a series in which the book may be published, and possibly a title entry. A classified catalogue, which
consists of entries arranged in the same order as the books
are classified and kept on the shelves, would provide the

main entry (author, as for the dictionary catalogue) at the book's classification number, and other added subject entries as necessary at appropriate classification numbers; in addition there would be brief entries for the editors etc., as mentioned for the dictionary catalogue, in one combined index, or preferably in separate indexes. The class number appears above the entry at either the right-hand or the left-hand side, every number commencing at exactly the same distance from the edge of the entry card or paper to aid immediate finding of the number. The left-hand side is best for card catalogues as the number is immediately above the author, and this saves time and eye fatigue looking for the author, but it must be at the right-hand side of an entry in a sheaf catalogue (a loose-leaf binder containing small sheets of paper). The classified catalogue brings all entries on one subject together, the individual entries at each number being arranged in alphabetical order of authors. Several entries by one author are arranged alphabetically by title, articles being ignored.

An advantage of the classified catalogue is that where the books are classified according to a bibliographical classification, entries for books on related subjects are close together; this is not the case with the dictionary catalogue where they may be in widely separated parts of the catalogue *and as there is no key or list of the headings* they can easily be overlooked. Every subject in a classified catalogue is indexed. This is a great advantage as the user can quickly and easily see what the whole stock of the library is on any subject, and its related subjects, without having to consult different parts of the catalogue.

All the entries are included in one alphabetical sequence in a dictionary catalogue, but in a classified catalogue, all entries other than subject entries will be in indexes (in effect they are separate catalogues). In practice the indexes to the classified catalogue, except the subject index to the classification, are sometimes combined in a 'name catalogue' for the number of title and series entries are relatively few in number compared with the author entries. Strictly speaking, a name catalogue is one in which the headings (under which entries are arranged) are of names of persons or corporate bodies.

Deciding on suitable subject headings and making proper subject references to these is the most difficult part of cataloguing and fails more examination candidates than any other part of the examination. Unfortunately, one cannot tell what subject-headings are likely to be provided in the catalogue, or in what order they will be, and although guide cards can do much to help the user find his way through the mass of cards, there will certainly not be a guide card for every subject-heading. In many cases there may be only two or three cards to each subject. Every card must be examined therefore to make sure that the subject required is not overlooked. This makes a dictionary catalogue an infuriating thing to use compared with a classified catalogue.

In the latter, the entries are arranged in classified order, and one can easily and quickly find the subject needed once one has discovered its appropriate number from the subject index to the classification. This is a much simpler kind of catalogue to compile and is much easier to use.

Another advantage of the classified catalogue over the dictionary catalogue is that the user can get an idea of the library's holdings on any particular subject so much more readily. Supposing one were consulting Dewey 796, outdoor games, all the cards at 796 and before 797 would indicate the library's holdings on this subject – squash, badminton, tennis, soccer, rugby, cricket, wrestling, fencing, etc. If one looked up the subject under the heading 'Outdoor sports' in the dictionary catalogue one would find only entries for books on outdoor sports in general, and be referred to all those headings under which one would have to look before having an idea of the library's total holdings on outdoor sports.

The disadvantages of the dictionary catalogue would not be so apparent in a children's library because of the fewer number of entries, but they would still exist. A child would find his way to, and through, the subject headings in a dictionary catalogue with more difficulty than he would in a classified catalogue where the subject index, which is easy to consult, would direct him to a specific number. For example, supposing a reader wished to know what books the library had on birds, he would have to look at the broad subject heading 'Birds' – and there might be several sub-divisions of this heading – as well as under the names of all the individual kinds of bird he could think of. The appropriate number would follow each name entry. The classified catalogue would have all the books on all kinds of birds listed between 598.2 and 598.9.

BOOK ORDERING AND PROCESSING

The routines carried out between the time of deciding to purchase a book until it is ready for the shelves are the responsibility of departments variously called Ordering, Cataloguing, and Processing departments according to the size of the library and the custom in the country concerned. Sometimes in very large libraries there are all three. In the smaller libraries, all these processes are carried out in a Cataloguing Department, or if the library is so small that very few books are purchased, they may be done as part of the routines of other departments. They are often duties which keep the staff busy in public departments because little demand is made on their time by members of the public. The carrying out of this work must be organized according to the size of the library and the emphasis which is placed

on certain aspects of the library's work. It is an advantage
from the point of view of efficiency and maintenance of a
high standard of performance if all children's processing
work is carried out by staff who specialize in it.

Ordering books
When it has been decided which books shall be added to
the library, it is desirable to check those it is intended to
purchase with the catalogue of books already in stock, and
also with the lists of books on order, so as to avoid ordering
unintentionally (a) books which are already in stock, and
(b) unrequired duplicate copies. The actual method of
ordering the books for the children's library would depend
very largely on the kind of library, the extent to which
centralization and departmentalization exists and also on the
size of the library. In a large library for example, where
cataloguing, classification and book processing are centralized for the whole system, the method of ordering children's
books must necessarily conform to the method used for
ordering adult books.

In modern library systems, continuous multiple stationery
is sometimes used for ordering books. This has very definite
advantages in that there is considerable economy of time and
effort, for where several records of books are required such
as, for a shelf-list, for the auditor, for the accessions register,
and for the master catalogue, these can all be provided from
one original typing, the various copies being obtained by
means of carbons inserted between the sheets of continuous
stationery. Thin paper is necessary, except that one sheet
(to be used as the master catalogue copy or as the accessions
record) may be of thicker paper and should be the bottom
one of the set. Continuous stationery is usually very expensive,
but the saving of time involved in making the different
records individually and the need to check *each* of them for
accuracy is worth the extra expense. As an alternative to

using the very long single-entry-width sheets usually supplied by the manufacturers of this kind of stationery, it is possible to use several sheets of perforated paper gummed together at the top on a securing strip outside the typing area. Sheets $33\frac{1}{2}$ inches by 10 inches can be perforated to give 22 pieces 5 inches by 3 inches, secured by half-inch strips gummed together at the top. These can be made up by any competent printer and can be inserted in an ordinary typewriter. Copies can be made by using carbons the same size as the sheets.

The diagram opposite indicates a suitable wording for an order slip of this kind. The slips on which the duplicate entries are made, and their purposes, are also represented. The name and address of the library would be fully printed where the dotted lines appear at the bottom of the slip unless books were to be delivered to different libraries for processing.

The top sheets of continuous stationery are printed fully, including a request to a bookseller to supply the book entered to a given address. The others only need have the purpose of the record printed on them, as: Audit, Accessions, Classified Catalogue, Master Catalogue; or they may be made of distinctive colours to indicate the various records.

Most libraries need at least three records – some more – for these different purposes, and it is an advantage to have them on separate slips of paper because the entries can then be arranged between selection and the end of processing in a variety of sequences, and re-arranged in different order as required. They can, for example, be arranged at different stages of the work under publisher, author, bookseller, or date of ordering; such adaptability is not possible with lists containing a number of entries. The chief advantage, however, of using slips of the standard 5 inch by 3 inch size, is that the entries can be arranged in groups to show the stage which the ordering has reached. For example, as soon as a decision has been made to order a book, an entry is

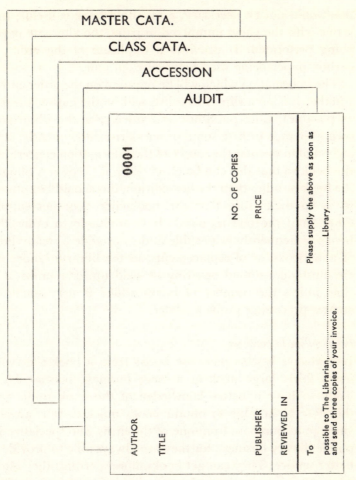

made on the appropriate 5 inch by 3 inch slip, and as the work proceeds the slips are moved behind guides such as 'On order', 'Received', 'Outstanding', 'Returned to bookseller', and then, as processing continues, they go into their permanent files.

If separate slips are not used, and in a very small library

85

this would not be necessary, a manifold book is useful; this is one with the pages numbered in pairs, the alternate pages being perforated. It provides a duplicate of the order, a carbon paper being used between each pair.

The information which will be required on the order entry, whether it is on a slip or in a list, will be the author (as full as possible), title, publisher and price. For the librarian's own guidance in case some queries arise subsequently, it is a good plan to enter the source of the information concerning the book so that this can be checked up if necessary. Should the book be other than the first edition, this should be entered so as to make sure that the bookseller does not supply other than the one required. It is advisable to order the books as frequently as possible and so provide a steady flow of new books, or of replacements, to the library. Under no circumstances should ordering be held up for months at a time unless the number of books added is very small: it creates processing problems later.

From whom to purchase

It is always best to purchase books from a bookseller who has a fairly large stock or a large business, because he is likely to have a better knowledge of the book trade and therefore to be able to obtain books quicker. It is an advantage to purchase from one of the firms who specialize in public library business, for they are always able to provide a better service. They can get books more speedily; they often carry large stocks themselves (and this is particularly important with children's books) and they order books in large quantities against anticipated sales. They often carry out the rebinding of books or casing books in special (sometimes plasticized) cases, or provide plastic jackets for books at very reasonable prices. It is a great financial saving to obtain books in a strengthened form so that the covers of the books may outlast the paper. This is seldom the case with books used in public libraries when supplied in publishers' cases.

If funds are extremely limited (it is not *essential* that books should be available in a children's library as soon as they are published), it often pays to buy ex-libris books from a circulating library, or 'subscription' library as they are sometimes called. The choice of titles is, however, extremely limited as far as children's books go, for there are only one or two circulating libraries which have a large stock of children's books. Sometimes certain titles can be bought at reduced rates from booksellers who specialize in library business and/or who have over-ordered some titles. Second-hand booksellers often have children's books at reasonable prices.

It is quite a common practice for most publishers to dispose of their remaining stock of a book which is not selling very well. Such surplus stocks are normally purchased by one or two firms who then sell them in fairly large numbers to second-hand booksellers, who in turn issue lists of such books at prices which are much less than the original published price. These books are known as remainders, and although the prices are quite reasonable, the libraries should make absolutely certain that the books are really necessary, or that they are good books, rather than purchase them simply because they are available at much lower prices than the original ones. Quite often remaindered books are on subjects which are not very popular, or for which there is little demand, or the books themselves may not be very good; the librarian therefore wants to make quite certain that they are worth buying. Incidentally, only a very small proportion of children's books are remaindered.

Receiving the books
The first process to be undertaken when the books are received from the bookseller, is to check them against the

87

bookseller's invoice to see that the right number of the correct editions has been supplied, and that the price has been entered on the account correctly. It used to be the practice to examine every book very carefully to make sure that it was not defective in any way, e.g. that sections were not omitted or had not been bound in upside down. A few books *are* defective but the amount of time spent examining large numbers of books is not justified by the few which are found to be faulty. Any defects will be noticed subsequently and faulty copies will be exchanged for good copies by the publishers, or credit given if the books are out of print, if sent back through the bookseller.

The Process Stamp. It is usual as soon as the book is checked off with the bookseller's invoice, to stamp the back of the title-page with the Process Stamp and to write in the appropriate place in this the name of the bookseller (usually abbreviated) and the published price, with the price paid – in brackets – if the book was published second-hand or at a price which was more than ten per cent less than the published price because it was a 'remainder' or for some other reason. The prices are often entered in code. Thus the books themselves contain enough information for them to be accessioned, and the accounts can be passed for payment immediately. The classifier puts the class number and the accessioning clerk the accession number in the appropriate places. The process stamp ensures that the information required to be recorded is entered, and also that it is placed in a uniform place on a part of the title-page that is not likely to be cut off when the book is re-bound.

Accessioning the books
Classifying and cataloguing the books is the next stage in the progress of the books to the shelves. They are then accessioned. If the books were ordered by separate slips, the

particular slip used as the accession slip is obtained from the sequence in which it was filed when the order was sent to the bookseller, and the accession number written on it in the top right-hand corner. If slips are not used, but some form of book (which may be an exercise book or a specially printed book) ruled with lines and columns for specific information, the appropriate details must be entered for every book, allocating one numbered line to every copy. Accessioning can absorb a great amount of time which can easily be saved if books are ordered on slips, and duplicates of these are used for the accessions record, for they will contain much of the information required for the purpose. Information which should be entered in any accessions record, or 'stock' record as it is sometimes called, is the author, title, date of publication, publisher and price, date of purchase, class number, source (i.e. name of bookseller or donor) and purchase price. Provision should also be made somewhere in the record for entering the date of withdrawing the book from circulation, and also for recording any subsequent replacement which may occur. The purpose of the accessions record is to provide a complete list of all the books in stock, in a numbered order, so as to keep a detailed record of the *number* of books in the library and to help trace particulars of individual copies which may be needed at some time, e.g. to determine how much to charge a reader for a lost book. It is necessary to keep a separate record of all books which are found to be missing or are withdrawn (whether they are replaced or withdrawn permanently from stock) so that at the end of the year the number of withdrawn titles can be deducted from the number of books added to stock and the net increase or decrease – and therefore the final stock figures of the year – obtained. The other main reason for keeping an accessions record, is to satisfy the auditor or any other authorized official that all books purchased have actually been put into stock, and that the librarian has been fulfilling his duties with proper responsibility.

If a work is in several volumes, an accession number must be given to each volume. For this purpose a separate slip is used for each, or a separate line if the accessions register is in book form. It is usual for the number of lines to a page of an accessions book to be printed with numbers nought to nine and for there to be fifty lines to a page; this is a help in quickly calculating the number of entries. The actual accession number is progressively increased of course, by adding appropriate tens, hundreds, and thousands figures before the printed figures.

It is desirable to have a record of the number of books in each main class of the classification in order to be able to maintain some sort of balance of stock. With the printed form of accessions register, this can be obtained by having a column for each main class and entering a stroke in the appropriate column, according to the class number of the book entered. At the bottom of the page, the number of strokes in each column is totalled up and cross-checked to make sure they total the number of lines to a page.

If slips are used for accessioning, the same result can be achieved by having a separate sequence of numbers for each main class, the class being distinguished by a letter to avoid confusion; the total number of books in stock in each main class is therefore automatically analysed at the end of the year. When it is required to know the number of books added during the year, all that is necessary is to ascertain the number of the last book accessioned and to deduct from this the number of the last book accessioned the year before. To determine the actual total stock, one adds to the previous year's total the number of books added during the year, and deducts from this the number of slips put on one side because of books withdrawn either for replacement or for cancellation.

Where accessioning is done on cards or slips of paper, and

books are 'charged' by accession numbers, this method has
advantages over that whereby continuous numbering is
used irrespective of subject classes, because the smaller
accession number resulting from the use of a separate
sequence of numbers for each main class of the classification makes it easier to charge and discharge books
when the Browne method is used. Charging symbols should
be as brief as possible, and this is one way of achieving
brevity.

For the same reason it is desirable when the accessions
register type of record is used, to use up accession numbers
of books withdrawn permanently from stock, allocating them
to new titles. Separate pages will have to be reserved for
numbers used up, otherwise the method of accessioning is
the same.

Preparing books for issue

A number of physical processes are normally carried out in
preparing books for issue; these include stamping, embossing,
perforating, labelling.

Stamping. Books are usually stamped with rubber stamps to
indicate ownership, although the extent to which this is done
varies considerably. The theft of books from libraries of all kinds
is quite common, and if rubber stamp impressions are made on
certain pages of all books it is easier to identify library books
in which attempts have been made to remove them. Should
a thief be caught, the publicity obtained from subsequent action
helps to reduce thefts. It is a common practice to stamp
books on particular pages, e.g., 1, 51, 101, 151 and so on,
the title-page and the last page, with a small round rubber
stamp $\frac{1}{2}''$ in diameter; the reason for using a round one
being that it always looks neat, whereas a square or oblong
stamp looks unsightly if it is not absolutely parallel with the
edges of the page. A top edge stamp is particularly useful as

this is extremely difficult to remove: it also has publicity value, for it is a permanent advertisement for the library. Stamping systematically on particular pages also ensures that a book is adequately stamped. In many libraries stamping is not now done as much as it used to be – in fact in some libraries books are not stamped at all. Consequently one often sees books from these libraries on second-hand book stalls. The reasons given for not stamping are (a) the cost of staff time in carrying out this work – a reason which applies less in developing countries, and (b) that stamping is not a deterrent to theft – a mistaken belief.

A perforator with a number of small needles arranged in the form of the library's name is sometimes used to punch the name through a page of a book. The type of press used for addresses on note-paper is often used to emboss the name of the library on book pages. With both these methods, one or more specific pages, not the first or last ones, should always be treated as a 'secret' mark.

A die press is used in many libraries to indent the name into the back and front covers of books. Some of these machines are heated electrically, and impress the name in gilt or metallic foil. This is a particularly useful means of marking ownership, for the name is always visible when a book is lying down.

Some librarians hold that if people wish to steal books they will do so whatever obstacles are placed in their way. To some extent this is true, but every obstacle makes it more difficult and is bound to help reduce theft. Children are no less liable than adults – in some countries at any rate – to steal books, and the librarian has a responsibility to protect books provided from public funds for the use of a community. These processes do not take an undue amount of time in relation to the protection they give and the years the books will remain in circulation. Moreover, this is unskilled work which can be done by manual workers or even helpers who should be enrolled in all children's libraries to assist the librarian in numerous ways. In view of the increasing cost of books it is even more important to reduce losses.

Labelling. Another simple operation is inserting labels in books. Labels are usually of two kinds: (a) an ownership, 'ex libris', or 'plate' label as it is variously called, which may vary from a small one with merely the name of the department or library printed on it to a much larger one containing a summary of the rules or facilities available, and (b) the date label. The ownership label is usually stuck down completely and may be pasted with gum, a thin paste, mucilage or a mountant which is put on with a small, fairly stiff round brush as is recommended on p. 100. A plastic 'brush' is not satisfactory as it does not spread the adhesive smoothly and is not so quick to use as a brush. It is usual to have the labels in a pile while pasting them, taking care to brush the adhesive across the edges, otherwise it will get onto the front of the labels. Gumming machines which have a small tank of gum built into them are very useful for labels if the whole surface is to be pasted.

Corner pockets to hold book cards, made in the same way as readers' tickets, are pasted down completely. A triangle of a single piece of card is not satisfactory as it comes away after much use.

The date label is placed on the second end-paper (the first free one), and the board label with the corner pocket below, opposite this on the inside of the front cover. Other positions are not satisfactory.

It has been assumed that the Browne book-charging method would be used, for this is the one most likely to be adopted in developing countries, as it requires no machinery and is simple to operate. The Islington adaptation of Browne, which is described on page 115, is equally suitable in such countries and only requires a small manually operated machine to print name and address slips. In many British libraries where photocharging or some other system involving the use of expensive electrically-operated machines is used for recording the loan of books from adult libraries, 'Browne' is used in the children's library.

Each book-charging method requires different stationery and therefore different book preparation.

Withdrawals

In order to keep an accurate record of the book stock, the number of 'withdrawals' (books taken out of circulation) as well as accessions must be recorded class by class. Where an accessions register is used, a separate list can be kept, or merely a note of the accession numbers of books withdrawn can be entered on a sheet of paper and the class analysis made by the method used for obtaining the progressive analysis of additions already described.

Where slips are used, the accession slip for a withdrawn book is put at the end of the sequence behind a 'withdrawn' guide, and its number is used immediately an additional book in the same class is to be accessioned. The account can be kept straight by recording on a separate analysis card at the end of the sequence, the *actual* accession number of a withdrawn book used up for a new title.

DEPARTMENTAL ROUTINES

The work of the children's library should be organized in such a way that all the routine work is carried out as soon as it is required to be done in order to keep the work up-to-date. This means that there must be an adequate staff. The timesheet should be so arranged that there are enough staff on duty at all times, not only to deal with the normal clerical routines, book processing and other work, but also to deal with the issue and return of books and yet have staff available to help children find the books or information they need. This last is the most important aspect of the day-to-day work of a children's librarian, apart from seeing that normal routines do not get behindhand. It is quite common in children's libraries for most of the books to be borrowed during rush periods when the children are returning home from school, especially if it is near the library. These rush periods can make the preparation of a satisfactory time-sheet a difficult business, especially in a small library where relief cannot be obtained from another department.

The daily routines include putting the books on the shelves in correct order, returning the books to the shelves throughout the day, writing notices requesting the return of overdue books, arranging displays, sorting and counting the records of books lent, entering the numbers in the issue statistics record, and making such reports to the Chief Librarian as are necessary.

Orderly books

To take these one by one, arranging the books in order should be the first call on the time of the junior members of the staff. It is essential, so as to make it easy to find the books required, that they should be checked for order and tidied on the shelves first thing in the morning. Then, as soon as the library is open for use, the children and staff will be able to go to any shelf and be sure of finding all the books available in a particular category in their right places. The correct replacement of returned books should continue throughout the day.

Overdue notices

Writing reminders to people that books have become over-due and requesting their return, is an essential routine which should be carried out daily. Many readers are apt to overlook the fact that they have books from the library, especially if they have read them and have put them on one side expecting to return them quickly but not being able to do so for one reason or another. In recent years there has been an increasing tendency to refrain from sending overdue notices to adults until a book has been in the hands of a reader for five or six weeks. This is either because it has been found that readers are aware that they have books out and do not intend to return them quickly and are quite willing to pay any necessary fines, or because the particular routine used in connexion with photographic and some other charging methods does not lend itself to writing 'overdues' sooner. Owing to the tediousness of reading microfilms, ten weeks is quite common with photographic charging.

The sending of reminders requesting the return of children's books should not be left so long, however, because they are usually much shorter than adult books and can be read in less time. Very often children who have kept books overdue and ask parents for money to pay the fines get into trouble with their parents for not returning the books earlier, and a prompt reminder helps to prevent this cause of friction, which sometimes results in children's ceasing to use the library. It is particularly important that subsequent overdue notices after the first should be sent out promptly at weekly intervals. Delay in sending these may mean considerable difficulty later in securing the return of the books.

In many children's departments of public libraries it is not the practice to send more than one or two notices to the member but to write to the head teacher of the school which the pupil attends asking for his co-operation in securing the return of the books. This is one reason why teachers are asked to sign children's membership cards. In some libraries this is not done until a much later stage in the efforts to secure the return of books, in order to avoid unnecessary bother to the head teachers. The most satisfactory stage at which this should be done can best be determined in the light of local conditions and the attitude of the head teachers towards the use of the library service. Fortunately, many head teachers look favourably on the children's library and do everything in their power to further co-operation between the library and the school, and are therefore quite willing to help secure the return of the books.

Book displays

Where book displays are arranged amongst the shelves they should be replenished, not only as a regular routine at the beginning of every day, but also throughout the day as it becomes necessary. This can be done without any inconvenience if the subjects of the display are fairly general ones, for suitable books returned by readers can be placed on them instead of being returned to their normal place on the shelves. The tidiness of these displays is important because a tidy library is a very much more attractive place than an untidy one; junior members of the staff should be trained to put books on display in an upright position (if they have been laid down by readers or are otherwise out of place) whenever it is necessary, as a part of their normal shelving routine.

Sorting the issue

The charges or other records of the day's issues should be sorted into order before the day's work ends if possible, if not, it should be done first thing the following morning. It is desirable that it should be a continuous process, kept up whenever there are a few moments to spare throughout the day. It is an advantage to sort Browne charges into pigeonholes as they are made, and to arrange them in strict order later. Such initial sorting can be done quite easily in this way and lessens the time taken with the final sorting into strict order.

The reasons for sorting into pigeon-holes in the first instance are (a) to speed up subsequent sorting by having large numbers of charges broken down into broad groups and (b) to enable progressive counting of loans to be done class by class. The pigeon-holes are labelled with the first symbol of the main classes of the classification, or the letters of the alphabet for fiction. Towards the end of the day, or when the bulk of the day's issues has been made, the charges are taken from the pigeon-holes and sorted into strict order, then those made as a result of books being issued later will be sorted into correct order as made. If the record of books issued can be made from the charges after they are finally arranged (that is if the fiction is kept separately from the non-fiction and the latter are arranged in order of the classification, and no more detailed record is required than can be obtained from the charges in this order) then there is no need to record the number of charges when they are taken from the pigeon-holes for sorting – they can be counted as soon as the day's issue has been finally arranged. But if the charges are arranged by authors' names or by accession, or some other number, yet a record of loans by class number (whether only main class or more detailed) is required, then the number of charges will have to be recorded on an issue sheet as they are taken from the pigeon-holes. Like all routines this work should be done as soon as possible, for any accumulation of duties can be a nuisance.

Routine reports

The preparation of weekly, monthly and quarterly reports required by the Chief Librarian should similarly be prepared as soon as it is possible to do so. In order that he may have some knowledge of the activities taking place and the amount of work being done in the children's library, weekly and monthly reports giving all kinds of details in addition to particulars of issues of books should be completed. This is particularly important in a system comprising several libraries as it helps him, and the supervising children's librarian, to know what work is being undertaken. The statistics help to show usage tendencies and give definite information which, when filed and compared with previous reports, are important when considering the effectiveness of past activities and proposals for new developments.

Physical condition of stock
As books are returned by borrowers they may with advantage be looked through quickly to see that they are in good condition and suitable for circulating again. Children sometimes write, scribble, or draw in library books, and examination of those returned, in the presence of the reader before he goes to the shelves, helps to prevent this pernicious practice which, if not checked, may become a menace. Every book which goes to the shelves with comments written in it serves as encouragement for someone else to do the same thing. Such writing should therefore be rubbed out or removed with ink eradicator.

Examination of the books in this way will also reveal portions cut or torn out by readers; this can become another and more serious menace, because books damaged in this way have to be replaced involving not only the cost of the books but also the cost of ordering and processing them – and this is quite considerable.

All books which need repair, new date labels inserted, re-binding or replacement, should be put on one side and dealt with as soon as pressure of work attending to borrowers permits. Such work should not be allowed to accumulate, for each individual repair takes only a few moments, and books should not be kept out of circulation longer than is necessary. The following day the task is more formidable.

Repairing books. Books can be made to last much longer once they begin to show signs of wear, or suffer damage, if they are repaired immediately. The following materials will be required: paste (fairly thin and not of the consistency of a mountant such as is used for photographs), gum, rolls of adhesive transparent paper, 'Sellotape' or some other make of transparent, adhesive 'tape', thin and soft transparent paper called 'Japanese' paper, a small brush with many bristles not more than half an inch long and fairly stiff. The round, short-bristle brushes made for applying Gloy paste are excellent. A paste can be made satisfactorily and cheaply by mixing ordinary flour (not self-raising) with water and heating it, stirring it and adding hot water as necessary, over a moderate heat until it becomes fairly thick. Oil of cloves can be added to prevent it going bad, and mercuric chloride[1] should be added to prevent silverfish and other insects eating it. Mercuric chloride is a very strong poison and is best used in tablet form, care being taken to see that no unauthorized person has access to it. Insects always go for the starch used in book-making, and mercuric chloride, or some similar ingredient, is incorporated by many book manufacturers in their processes, especially in books largely intended for use in tropical countries.

Torn pages. The neatest method, but one that takes time and trouble, is to charge a brush fairly generously with paste and, using the side of the brush, place a little, but not so much that it will spread, on each edge of the tear. Place a piece of Japanese or tissue-paper underneath the repaired

[1] The Crown Agents' Standard Specification No. 40 (1937, revised 1954) recommends: Copper sulphate in the proportion of 1 ounce to 2 gallons shall be added to the water used in making the paste or glue for binding, and powdered alum in the proportion of 1 ounce to 15 pounds shall be added to the finished adhesive. In addition there shall be added to the adhesive a solution of mercuric chloride and beechwood creosote in such proportions that the mercuric chloride shall constitute 2 per cent and the beechwood creosote 1 per cent of the total solid ingredients of the adhesive.

page and a piece on top, and close the book; leave for twenty-four hours in a letter press or under a weight and then remove the tissue-paper, taking great care if any paste has stuck to it, to remove it along the tear, not across, otherwise it may be reopened. The tissue paper will not stick to the page, unless too much paste has been used.

Loose illustrations and pages. These should be replaced by drawing the side of a lightly filled paste-brush along the edge of the page so as to leave a narrow strip, about $\frac{1}{16}$ inch thick, of thin paste. The least possible amount should be used or too much of the page will be stuck down. As some pastes are difficult to spread satisfactorily, one method of ensuring that a narrow strip of just enough paste is applied all along the edge is to lay the loose page on an old newspaper or magazine with a piece of fairly thick paper over it masking all but $\frac{1}{16}$ inch of it; the paste brush should be drawn diagonally across the exposed edge. The brush should never be drawn *down* the edge of a guard when used in this way (or down a number of date labels which have been fanned out to expose about $\frac{1}{16}$ inch of each edge) but across, or the paste may spread where it is not required. Guards must always be used with thick and hard pastes and also with very thin ones. The leaf opposite the loose one in the section should be examined to see if it also is loose.

Broken joints. If the mull or gauze which secures the sections to the cover has not been broken, a little paste or gum can be spread down the joint; this will have the effect of sticking the endpaper to the cover. A piece of tough thin paper or adhesive linen could be stuck all the way down the joint. This is the best method to employ if the mull has been broken. Should the whole of the mull be broken, an edge of paste down the spine at the joint would be helpful before repairing the joint.

Torn or broken spine. It is seldom possible to make a really good or permanent repair of the spine as the material is almost sure to come away again with handling. A thin paste with good adhesive qualities is in most cases better than a thick paste as it is easier to get it into places which are inaccessible to brushing. If a paper backing is missing from the folds of the sections this should be renewed. The repair may need 'packing up' with several layers of thick paper (but see that no paste remains on the surface of the spine or it will stick to the packing) and tying with string until dry. The same methods are used whether the covering material is paper, cloth or leather.

Other defects. Should the sewing of any section be broken, the back of the book broken, or the binding worn away as distinct from being torn, or there be several defects, not much can be done in the way of repairs and the book must be rebound.

Stains. Ink can be removed with an ink-eradicator, instructions for use being given on the container. Grease and oil may be removed by placing clean white blotting-paper on both sides and applying a hot iron, using fresh blotting-paper as necessary. Mud on the binding can be washed off with a little soapy water and rinsed, and the book stood in the open air to dry; as little water as possible should be used. Pencil marks should be rubbed gently with an india-rubber; if the fibres of the paper are roughened, rub down with the thumbnail. A soft art rubber should be used, or the surface of the paper may be roughened too much. Cleaning the paper with soapy water to remove stains is not altogether satisfactory as the paper has to be rinsed with clean water and dried; this inevitably weakens the paper somewhat and it is almost sure to become cockled. A bleach is sometimes effective but this may cause the paper to deteriorate.

Re-binding

Books in libraries, especially public libraries, are subjected to considerably more wear than most books. It is necessary therefore that their bindings should be much stronger than the cases put on them by the publisher. In order to cater for the needs of public libraries, a number of firms have specialized in library binding which is quite distinct from other forms of binding craftsmanship. Among the special features of library binding are: (a) the outside and inside leaves of each section sometimes even alternate leaves, are guarded with serrated edge guards (if the paper is of poor quality and straight edged guards are used, the pages may tear away at the guard edges); (b) all sections are sewn on to from three to six tapes according to the size of the book; (c) the tapes are securely fixed to the boards which should be split to take them; (d) joints are of linen or very tough paper; (e) endpapers are of tough paper; (f) the cloth used is waterproof, fadeless and fairly thick.

In recent years cheaper methods of binding fiction, children's books, and books not likely to be used very much, have been developed. These have used the minimum of materials and labour, and are based on the use of new adhesives; one method (the so-called 'perfect' binding) has the folds of the sections cut away and the resulting loose pages held together by adhesive. In countries where tropical or semi-tropical conditions of great heat and/or humidity occur books bound by such methods should be used cautiously as it has been found that this is not a satisfactory way of making, or re-binding, books.

Avoiding re-binding

Most library binders, and some booksellers who specialize in supplying books to public libraries, are having new books specially bound, sometimes in plastic-covered cases. In nearly all instances the books are bound from the sheets supplied by the publishers instead of being the ordinary publishers' editions re-bound. They incorporate methods for meeting the special needs of public libraries, and in most cases the jacket, or the decorative cover of the book (if it is published with a pictorial cover instead of with a plain cover with a loose jacket) is covered with transparent plastic secured to the book cover by heat. Books where the plastic has been secured to the outside of the cover, over its whole surface, are preferable to those where plastic has been stretched over the cover and secured only on the inside. Some firms' materials, methods and workmanship are better than others', but they are all worth considering. They are very economical for the library for the following reasons: (a) the initial cost of the strengthened or re-bound book is little above the published cost of the book, (b) the binding will generally outlast the paper and so re-binding costs are saved, (c) the work involved in writing instructions for the binder, recording books sent for binding, checking binding on return and labelling after re-binding (although this is done by the binder usually for a small charge), can be avoided. These costs in terms of salaries can be a considerable item.

Another advantage is that the books are not out of circulation while they are being re-bound – and (a very important item if the bindery is overseas) freight charges are avoided.

Plasticized jackets. If books cannot be purchased already re-bound, or with plasticized covers, the covers can be made to last much longer and the cost of re-binding often avoided by inserting the jackets of new books in plastic sleeves and securing them to the books in such a way that they cannot be easily removed. Sleeves with linen sewn along the top and bottom edges should be avoided. The most suitable kind of plastic jacket is that in which the plastic is secured to two wide strips of brown paper and is usable on jackets of different sizes.

Replacement or discarding?

When books have become worn out consideration has to be given to the need to replace them with another copy of the same title or with a different book. There are several factors involved here, the chief of which is the usefulness and popularity of the book. The first question to be asked is: was it constantly on loan? If it was, then replacement is justified. If it had been issued a minimum of twelve times a year in a highly literate country, replacement would still be justified. The frequency of issue can be determined by examining the date labels or the issue cards or record cards if details are entered every time a book is lent. No consideration need be given to the number of copies on the shelf as the number of issues will be fewer as a book loses its popularity. In the case of non-fiction other factors have to be considered; for example, is the book up-to-date? do other books deal with the same subject more satisfactorily? or are there other books with equally good text but better illustrations? is the subject one of general or continuing interest? One cannot expect non-fiction books to be read as much as story-books (although the use of this category of books by children is much greater than by adults) so the number of issues as a guide to replacement should be lower than in the case of stories. The figures of loans mentioned above would be for a busy library in a country where the habit of reading has become well-developed. In a library which was used less, the number of issues per annum to justify replacement would be smaller. Consideration of replacement is given as soon as the book is withdrawn from circulation, and the replacement routine put into operation immediately so as to prevent the availability of books becoming poorer than need be. Copies of titles not replaced would be discarded and all records for the individual copies cancelled; catalogue entries would be withdrawn in the case of the last copy of a title.

ISSUE METHODS

Records of issues are kept so as to know what books are on loan and to whom, and to be able to recall the books if necessary; also, incidentally, to keep an account of the number of books issued. One usually wants to know who has a particular book rather than what books a certain person has; the means of determining this will be described after dealing with the registration of readers.

Maintaining a register of members
Before arrangements can be made to record issues of books it is desirable to have a record of members of the library. Application cards or forms should be filled up by all those who wish to use the library, and they should be signed with the applicant's usual signature. Making formal application for membership helps the children to realize that only those who are admitted as members may use the library, and if the form of application has reference to keeping the library rules they will also realize they have some obligations. They should be told of the conditions of borrowing books (the number they are permitted to borrow at a time, the period allowed for reading, any fines which may be levied because of non-return in the time allowed, arrangements for renewal of loans and facilities for reserving books), and if the library is able to print introductions or guides to the library service for children they should be given a copy. On joining they should be taken to the shelves and shown where the most suitable books for their age group are kept, and how they are arranged, not omitting to tell them to ask the assistants

for any help they may need at any future time in finding books or information.

The first paragraph of the card is usually a request to join the library and an undertaking to obey the library rules. Information to be entered will be the child's date of birth, home address and school attended. The addresses are required so as to know how to communicate with him directly or through his school, should this be necessary, to secure the return of overdue books, as well as to be able to keep proper records which are useful when considering the use made of the library by children of certain ages, attending particular schools or kinds of schools, or living in particular areas.

There should also be provision, preferably at the back of the membership card, for the head of the school which the applicant attends to sign a recommendation that the applicant is considered to be a person who will benefit from the use of the library, and also for the parent or guardian to sign an undertaking to be responsible for any books borrowed by the applicant. The following are suitable wordings for a simple application for membership card.

X X X X PUBLIC LIBRARIES

I wish to belong to the Junior Library.   I promise to obey the regulations, look after my books, and return them to the library promptly.

NAME IN FULL...

ADDRESS ....

SCHOOL ....

DATE OF BIRTH........................   **DATE**..

PLEASE WRITE PLAINLY IN INK   **DO NOT FOLD THIS CARD**

RECOMMENDATION BY A PARENT OR HEAD TEACHER

I consider (name) ....

is capable of using the Junior Library and caring for books.

....
SIGNATURE OF PARENT OR HEAD TEACHER   DATE

ADDRESS ....

....

If it is desired to obtain a guarantee from the parent or guardian, the reverse of the card can provide for this in addition, 'I, e.g., ..., undertake to be responsible for all books borrowed by the applicant named on the other side' followed by a space for the guarantor's address.

Apart from the signatures, the cards may be completed by printing in by pen or by using a typewriter: handwriting is not essential, except for the signature. From the information given on the application card, membership tickets can be made out. The simplest way to regulate the issue of books to children is to issue tickets on which only one book may be borrowed at a time. The number of tickets will depend on several factors such as the number of books in the library in relation to the potential number of borrowers, the distance at which the borrowers live from the library, and the extent to which it is desired to encourage the use of the library. It will be appreciated that if the library has only a small collection of books and a potentially large number of readers it may be desirable to restrict the number of tickets per reader. It would be preferable to increase the number of books available, but if this is not possible, the fewer tickets they have, the oftener they are likely to come to the library to change books, and consequently there will be a larger number of books on the shelves for other people to choose from. On the other hand, if a large number of the members live a long distance from the library it would be a disservice to give them only one or two tickets, for obvious reasons.

If tickets are lost, members should be required to fill up a form requesting duplicate tickets, and in doing so to undertake (a) to return to the library the duplicates should they find the originals, and (b) to be responsible for any books which might be borrowed by other people on their original tickets.

It is desirable in a children's library to get the members to re-register every second year. This helps to keep the records up-to-date and ensures that they relate only to 'live' members (that is people who are using the library or may have used it during the past two years). It also ensures a reasonably accurate record of the schools, and also the kind of schools, which borrowers attend; this helps the librarian to know in which schools publicity might be undertaken. Particulars of the approximate number of children of different ages who are members of the library can be compiled from these records. This information is extremely useful when selecting books, because one has accurate statistics of how many borrowers there are of each age.

Any library system, especially a developing one, needs to have all the statistical information it can obtain with regard to its members, and this can be obtained easily if the required data appears on the membership cards. The use of punched card sorting machines is desirable in order to obtain analyses of this information. The membership card should be so designed that the information for analysis is recorded in such a way that it can be coded quickly by clerks for the operators who punch the statistical cards, which are fed through the analysing machines. The wording on pages 112–13, indicates the way such a card can be designed. The analysis of membership can indicate the number of members of each race, linguistic and age group joining any particular library, where they live and where they go to school. This is very useful in revealing where additional library services are needed, what age groups should be most catered for at each library, what type of schools and which schools (or which geographical group of schools) children attend. Children's reading interests can also be analysed, although this kind of information, when given by the applicants, may not always be very reliable. Many cities throughout the world have problems in library provision in that the community includes several races, and therefore books in various languages are needed. The extent of the problem in this respect can be statistically gauged from the cards. It is not easy to complete such a card, but a printed guide to completing the forms was issued to every applicant at Singapore, where such cards were used, and the staff were naturally willing to help.

Before the tickets are made out the file of members' application cards should be checked to see that tickets are not already in existence.

If a typewriter is not used, tickets are best made out with waterproof ink, such as india or engrossing ink, so that it will not smudge or 'run' if the tickets get wet. The use of such ink helps to reveal any unauthorized alterations made by members. The information on the ticket would consist of the name, address, telephone number, school attended, the member's number (if any), and the number of tickets issued. The last is useful if a variable number of tickets are issued, to assist in the correct replacement of a lost ticket should this become necessary. The date of expiry would be stamped on the ticket.

Should members change their address they should notify

the librarian who would enter the new address on the member's original application form as well as on the tickets. Changes of address are best notified to the librarian on a form kept for the purpose saying that 'I, ... hereby notify my change of address and shall be glad if you will alter your records accordingly.' This can then be filed with the original.

Methods of issuing books

It is an advantage if the same method of issuing books is used in the children's department as in the adult, unless the adult department uses photocharging or some other method which permits the borrowing of an unlimited number of books, and makes it difficult to send overdue notices when the books are two or three weeks overdue.

(*a*) *The Browne method.* The method of issuing books which has been used in England for many years is the Browne system. This consists of inserting a book-card, provided for every book, in a reader's pocket ticket when the book is borrowed. In other words, the borrower has the ticket when he has no book out, and the book contains a book-card when it is not in the hands of a reader but in the library. When a reader wishes to borrow a book he hands in his ticket and the book-card is taken from the book and inserted in the ticket. When the book-card and ticket have been 'married' in this way, the charge (as the 'marriage' is called) is put on one side until later in the day when all the charges are arranged in some pre-determined order and the guide bearing the date when the books are due for return is placed in front of them.

The book-card kept in the book is $1\frac{3}{4}$ inches wide and 4 inches deep. This is kept in a pocket in a book when it is not on loan: the pocket is a piece of manilla about $3\frac{1}{2}$ inches wide folded in half and stuck together with one side open,

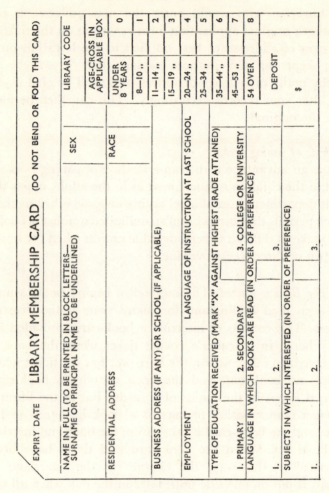

Front and reverse sides of application for membership c
centering particulars than is shown, for the card is $7\frac{1}{4}'' \times$

and is about 3 inches high. It is the same size and shape as
the reader's ticket and is pasted on the inside of the front cover

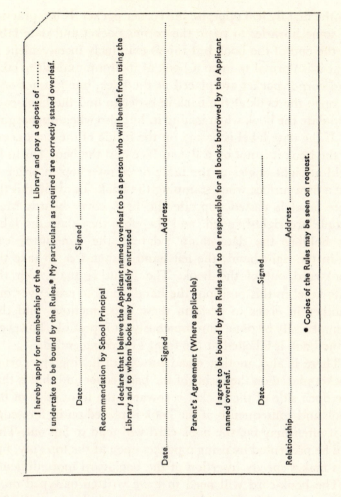

I hereby apply for membership of the .... Library and pay a deposit of ....
I undertake to be bound by the Rules.* My particulars as required are correctly stated overleaf.

Date.................. Signed ....

Recommendation by School Principal

I declare that I believe the Applicant named overleaf to be a person who will benefit from using the Library and to whom books may be safely entrusted

Date.................. Signed.................. Address..................

Parent's Agreement (Where applicable)

I agree to be bound by the Rules and to be responsible for all books borrowed by the Applicant named overleaf.

Date.................. Signed.................. Address..................

Relationship..................

* Copies of the Rules may be seen on request.

l by both adults and children. More space is given for conforms to the standard size for a punched card system.

of a book and as close to the joint as possible. The date label, on which the date due for return is stamped, is pasted

113

on the first fly leaf opposite the corner pocket. It is a practice in some libraries to paste the corner pocket and date label at the end of the book but this is extremely inconvenient in that it is normal to open a book at its front, and if the label and corner pocket are placed at the back, one has not only to open the book at the back in order to find the book-card and date the book when issuing it, but also when discharging it. If the date label is pasted on the inside of the back cover of the book it is not on a flat surface and the book has to be held at right angles to the table or counter top in order to get a firm surface when stamping the book. To avoid this the date label is pasted opposite the back cover board. Most people are right-handed, and therefore they date the label by holding the date-stamp ('dater', the Americans call it) in the right hand; the left hand is then free to take the book-card out of the book. The result is that, with the date label in this position, the hands have to cross over one another in order to perform these two functions, and this cannot easily be done simultaneously. It *is* possible, however, if the book is labelled at the front as recommended.

There is also another disadvantage of having the corner pocket placed on the inside of the back cover and that is that the open side of the pocket is towards the front edge of the book and consequently if the book is placed on its fore-edge as it often may be, the book-card will tend to fall out. This can be prevented by using a pocket open at the top only, but this makes speedy insertion of the book-card more difficult.

The book-card will need to have written or typed on it the author, title, accession number and, if a non-fiction book, its class number. The order in which this information appears on the book-card will depend on the symbols used for charging the books. If they are charged by the accession number, this must appear at the top of the book-card, but if by the author's name then *this* must appear at the top. This matter is dealt with more fully later.

The reader's pocket ticket, which should be made of manilla of medium weight, is made in exactly the same way, and is the same size, as the corner pocket. In addition to having written on it the personal details of the member as previously mentioned, it will be necessary to print on it such other information as the name of the library and any conditions of membership, or of the use of the ticket such as 'not transferable', 'non-fiction', etc.

The date labels (or date due slips as they are sometimes called) should not be pasted along the top edge, but along the edge nearest the joint of the book and placed about ¼ inch from the joint. If pasted on the other edge, they will cockle with use.

The main disadvantage of the Browne method – the time taken to discharge books – has been eliminated by the Islington method which was introduced in 1964.[1] This is just the same as 'Browne' except that book-cards are 'married' to expendable name and address slips which the readers make themselves. The method requires the provision of small machines into which readers can insert their membership cards (plastic with embossed name and address) and print as many copies of their name and address as they wish. These are handed in when books are stamped, and each is placed with a book-card in a corner pocket. When the books are returned the discharge of the loan may occur immediately, or it may be delayed until a convenient time, the name and address slip being destroyed. All the advantages of the Browne method remain plus that of the avoidance of queues when people return books – and this is the only objection ever levied against Browne. The only disadvantage of the Islington method may have in a children's library is the lack of any restriction on the number of books on loan to

---

[1] *See* Elliott, C.A. The Islington book charging system, *L.A.R.* 67(2), Feb. 1965, pp. 55-59.

any one reader at a time. With Browne, this is controlled by the number of tickets issued to each member.

There have been several other developments in the methods of issuing books since the last war and a number of libraries are now using microphotography and sometimes microphotography in association with punched cards. It has yet to be proved that these methods have advantages over the very simple Browne method let alone the Islington adaptation. It is rather a condemnation of microphotography that having introduced a modern mechanical method such as this in order to improve upon an existing method, one then may have to introduce some other expensive mechanical means, such as punched cards, in order to supplement it because of the amount of time taken by manually sorting the returned transaction cards. It is very similar to the proverbial use of a steam-roller to break a nut.

It has also yet to be proved by independent and unbiased examination of issue methods whether any one method is either more speedy or more economical than any other, and it is quite likely that if the microphotograph systems used with or without punched cards are carefully costed it will be found that they are much more expensive in terms of staff salaries and materials than the simple Browne method. The reason for this is that more operations have to be performed, and expendable materials such as microfilm and punched cards purchased. For my part, there is no question whatever that when all the routines are taken into consideration and costed, issuing books by the Browne or Islington methods is quicker and cheaper than any other.

The chief advantages of the Browne system are its simplicity of operation and the fact that all the information one needs for recording or discharging loans, as well as for the writing of overdue notices is provided at the time of issuing the books, and is immediately available at all times. This is not the case with the Newark system or any method based on, or resembling it, or with the microphotographic methods. In some libraries where photocharging is in use, people have to wait just as long, or longer, to have their books issued to them if there is only one microfilming machine or only enough staff to operate one. The amount of time spent queueing where the Browne method is used is really not very great and is largely dependent on the number of staff who are available at busy periods to discharge books. It is a question not only of the total number of staff employed, but also the planning of the staff time sheet. The actual time taken to discharge a book is seldom longer than twenty seconds, but the disadvantage occurs when there are several borrowers returning their books at the same time, and in large or busy libraries there may be as many as twenty-five people wishing to do this. All libraries are faced with the problem of rush periods in just the same way as are all shops, and the only solution to the problem seems to be to provide enough staff to cope with people at rush periods. Other relatively minor criticisms are that (a) as many tickets have to be issued as the number of books borrowers are permitted to have at a time, and (b) owing to the human element which is always supreme in the issuing and discharge of books, mistakes may occur. With regard to (a) this is in itself an advantage if it is necessary to place a restriction on the number of books a borrower may have out at one time. An unlimited number of books can only be permitted when the stock is so large as not to be unduly depleted by borrowings. Control of borrowings is desirable and is even necessary in a children's library, for some children will borrow whenever they feel inclined without bothering to return the books they already have out (they will also lend them without discrimination to their friends), and this may lead to trouble with their parents when asked for money to pay fines or when overdue books cannot be found. With regard to (b) mistakes can be largely avoided if staff are properly trained in their routines and develop accuracy as a part of responsibility, and if there is adequate supervision by senior members of the staff. Mistakes can occur with the photographic or any other method of recording loans.

(b) *The book-card method.* This is a simpler method which can be used in very small libraries, or in classroom libraries, or where the number of books issued is so small that time can be afforded for the readers to write their names at the time of borrowing books. The book-cards are 3 " wide by 5 " deep and are kept in a pocket similar to the one described for the Browne method. The card bears the same information as does the book-card in the Browne method, that is, author, title, accession number, class number if non-fiction, and is ruled with vertical columns for the insertion of the borrower's name, date due, and date returned. Whenever a borrower wishes to borrow a book he just writes his name on the card, and hands it to the librarian who dates it and the date label with the date due for return. When the book is returned, the librarian takes the card out of the sequence in which it is filed and stamps the date of return. The borrower is then able to go to the shelves and choose another book.

There is no limit to the number of books a person may borrow at a time with this method, unless a membership card is deposited in the library (and is filed in alphabetical order) as an indication that the member named thereon has a book out, or unless a book were not issued until one previously borrowed had been returned.

Instead of using a book-card, a reader's card could be used, putting the member's name, address, school or class, on the card and using the name as a filing symbol. The card would then be ruled for book number, date due and date returned.

With both these methods, the records of loans would be kept behind the appropriate date guides (the name of the month appearing in front of the first date guide for the month) and each sequence would be sub-divided by guides to help the assistants find the required charges quickly.

Whatever form of book-card is used, the charging symbol will need to be written by hand boldly and distinctly at the top, using waterproof ink. This is particularly important in countries where moist fingers may tend to smudge the characters, particularly if plastic book-cards are used. The characters should be ⅜ inch high. The author's surname should appear next (providing this is not used as the charging symbol), followed by the initials on the same line. Then would appear the title, abbreviated if possible to one line – or at most one and a half. Then the publisher's name on the next line. The publisher's name is important for if the book is to be replaced, it will be necessary to give the bookseller this information. Replacement orders will be made up from the book-cards as these are available and are the most convenient form of record to handle. The class number can go at the top right-hand corner or in any other convenient position.

If a spirit duplicator is used for making the catalogue entries this can be used to produce the book-cards also. In this case the information will appear up the length of the card and all that will have to be written by hand will be the charging symbol. It is an advantage to use any available mechanical apparatus for any of the library records, as it saves considerable staff time, ensures consistency and accuracy, and avoids checking work at each stage.

(c) *The register method*. This method is suitable in a class-room, or a library, or a department of a library, where the number of books issued is extremely small The exercise book is ruled with vertical columns in which the librarian, or the reader, writes name of borrower, date of issue (or date due for return), author, title, accession number, and date returned. This method is commonly used in unstaffed libraries.

An assessment of the three methods

The desirable aspects of any method of recording the loans of books are that it must be speedy at all stages (to avoid the formation of queues), simple, and not necessitate writing by the borrower or by the librarian. If the method is a simple and speedy one it will encourage the reading of books and discourage the borrowing of books without their loan being recorded, which may happen if children have to wait a long time for the book to be issued to them once they have made their choice. If many books have to be issued in a short time, (this is often necessary in a school or in a public library which many children visit during the lunch-hour or on their way to and from school), it is particularly important to use a very quick method to avoid the children having to wait long.

The Browne method. This widely-used method has the advantages of being simple, speedy, and not requiring writing to be done either by borrower or by librarian. It is very suitable for use in very small libraries and also in large ones. Where strict control is also desirable this method is admirable. One of its chief advantages is that the borrower of any book can be quickly traced, and if the book is required urgently for another reader he can immediately be asked in writing to return it.

The book-card method. The chief disadvantage of this method is that it requires (a) the date of issue or return to be written or stamped on the book-card as well as on the date label, and (b) the name of the applicant, and in the case of a school library, the borrower's class, to be written on the book-card every time a book is borrowed. It is not suitable in a public library or in countries where names are very similar and often recur in exactly the same or very similar form as do Chinese, Indian and Malay names. It is only suitable for a very small library. Other disadvantages are: there is no address of the borrower and consequently confusion may arise; writing may be illegible (this can be overcome if the librarian examines the card every time a book is borrowed to make sure that the name is clearly written), and it gives opportunity for unscrupulous borrowers to enter the name of someone else rather than themselves on the card.

The register method. This is one of the oldest methods of recording the loan of books. It is simple and needs very little in the way of equipment, only an exercise book being used. It is consequently an inexpensive method. No time is involved in filing the records of loans such as is necessary with methods (a) and (b). In a busy library the method is quite unsuitable because of the amount of time taken in recording the entries and also because there is only one register in which all borrowers have to write the many details required. It is natural that such details may be written hastily, and consequently very probably illegibly; also there is no supervision, as there is with the other methods, to make sure that the entries are both legible and correct. It has the further disadvantage that when wanting to secure the return of overdue books, every page of the register has to be examined to see that all the entries have had the 'date returned' column completed. This is also a disadvantage of method (b). In this connexion, method (a) shows up the overdue books automatically because the charges representing loans are arranged in systematic order behind the appropriate date guide which, by its very existence in the tray, indicates that there are books overdue.

It will be obvious that the size and use of the library will determine the suitability of a particular method of recording the loan of books. Where the number of books is small and the question of dishonesty does not arise, methods (b) and (c), the book-card and the register methods, are satisfactory.

With none of these methods is it necessary to have a trained librarian to issue the books; the work can be done by librarians in training, by 'helpers', or by senior pupils in schools.

The filing of loan records
With both methods (a) and (b) it is necessary to file either the charges or the book-cards in a predetermined sequence, either by accession number, or by author. It is much quicker to arrange charges in order and also to find those required when the books are returned, if the charges are arranged in *numerical* order. Figures are easier to recognize and to arrange than letters, particularly by people whose mother tongue is not English, largely because there are only nine of them as against twenty-six letters of the alphabet. The great disadvantage of arranging by accession numbers is that when particular books are reserved by members, one has got to refer to the catalogue or some other record in order to find the number of the book before the search through the charges can commence. This however is less trouble than making out a list of all books reserved and checking every book as it is returned with the list, which is the method that has to be used when the record of loans is made by photographic and other methods where a record of the borrower and of the book borrowed *cannot be seen at the time of discharging the book.*

These are the two methods which are normally used for filing loan records; the reason for keeping the charges, or book-cards, in both these methods, in groups according to the dates when the books are due back is to show up automatically overdue books as soon as they become overdue.

Arranging books by date does slow down the time taken searching for books which may be required because they have been reserved, but it has the merit of keeping records of books on loan in relatively small sequences, and this would not be the case if each day's records had to be inserted in a larger sequence by name of borrower or author. It also saves the time taken in sorting into a larger sequence. Finding records in a short sequence also takes less time than finding them in a long sequence. These short sequences simplify the writing of overdue notices as a daily routine which is essential in a public library in order to secure the prompt return of overdue books. Where books are lent for a longer period than two weeks and there are other means of securing their return, as in a school, the desirability of having the loan records in short sequences is not so great.

TEACHING THE USE OF THE LIBRARY

There is little point in providing a suitable building, a stock of appropriate books and a competent staff, unless the children are trained to make the utmost use of the facilities provided. Something more than letting them wander around on their own is desirable. They need to be told about the books in the library and how to make the best use of them. A brief informal look around on their first visit may be enough perhaps, especially for the youngest children. But for those over about nine years of age there should be formal talks to groups of from eight to a whole class. These children should be told the way books are made, how they can be damaged by careless handling, how the books in the library are classified and catalogued, and what facilities are provided. The talks may be provided in both a public library and in a school library where it is easier to organize them. Even though the number of staff in children's libraries may be inadequate, time devoted to talks is well spent and bears good dividends in the form of more worth-while use of the library.

The following extracts from 'Teaching the use of books to pupils in a secondary modern school with particular reference to the third and fourth years.' by P. M. Cadge, published in *Education Libraries Bulletin*, Summer 1959, by the University of London Institute of Education, emphasizes the importance of this work.

'Education is concerned with the development of a child as an individual and a member of a community. It should seek to develop a child's mental, spiritual, and physical powers within that child's capacity. It should cultivate the faculty of criticising and judging. A child should be helped to form valuable tastes and interests, and trained in a sense of social responsibility . . .

'The world is changing very rapidly indeed, and much information becomes out of date very quickly . . . Surely the important thing is the ability to be able to look up information when needed, and this involves knowing where to look and which books to consult for specific knowledge . . . Also, in these days when the popular newspapers tend to sensationalise the news, it is important that they learn to distinguish between fact and opinion and be able to compare different sources of information.

' . . it is vital that pupils be guided in using their leisure time wisely and develop interesting hobbies . . .

'If we are to succeed in these ideals, we must have plenty of books, attractive ones which appeal, and a room in which to put them. Hence a school library is an absolute necessity in the school of today, and if a full and proper use is to be made of the library, there is a strong case for teaching library skills somewhere during the school curriculum. There are three main problems . . . how much teaching should be given, when and by whom.

'Educational psychologists tell us that learning takes place most completely when the need arises. It would seem therefore, that library tools should not be taught until the need for them is felt. If however instruction is delayed, or becomes too informal, much time will be wasted for the same question will keep recurring throughout the class. On the other hand, if instruction becomes merely an academic exercise, it will lack a sense of purpose, the pupil will become disinterested and the teaching will be of little use. Therefore while a systematic course seems to be necessary, each piece of work should have a definite aim. While learning the necessary skills, the pupil should at the same time be practising them by searching for information connected with the work of the school or her own individual interests. Practical application should go hand in hand with instruction and drill. As the teacher librarian will be unable to give all classes in the school this instruction, her main role besides buying books and organizing the library, will be to draw up schemes of work and tender advice to colleagues on teaching methods, and to prepare practical aids.'

The handling of books

When children are first formally introduced to the use of books in a school, or when they visit the public library in classes from school, or if the children's librarian can get a group of children round her to interest them in the make-up and use of books, they should be taught how to handle books without damaging them. They can be shown too, how books are made by exhibiting a book which has come to pieces in the course of use. Such books will demonstrate, if in publishers' cases, the way the books are put together. They will also indicate how the sections are 'blacked' at the back in order to help the gatherer when collecting the sections for sewing, and whether they have been collected in correct order, one copy of each section without duplication. If a sheet of printed paper can be obtained from a publisher or a bookseller's or publisher's wrapping and folded to form a section, this will demonstrate the way printed pages are set out on a sheet of paper and printed before folding. A few diagrams kept on one side for this purpose will indicate the varieties of layout and folding. If it is not possible to accumulate several different sections, the fact that publishers' cases are secured to the sections forming the book simply by a piece of mull and an end-paper, or in some cases an end-paper only, will enable a 'cased' book to be taken to pieces and so help the children to appreciate how easy it is for books to become loose in their cases. If there are in the library any books with a broken or bent top of the spine, they can be used to demonstrate that books should not be withdrawn from the shelves by pulling on the cloth of the spine, but by pressing the index finger on the top edges of the book and levering it forward by a downward, and at the same time forward, pressure; then when there is enough of the book sticking out, beyond the books on either side, it can be gripped with the thumb and the remaining fingers and withdrawn without damaging the binding. Another method practised by some people, and even recommended by some librarians, is to push the books on either side of the one which is required with fingers and then grip the book. This however tends to cause unnecessary wear on the bottom edges of the boards of the adjoining books and also makes the shelves look untidy.

Children should be told that the proper way to mark their place is to put a thin card or piece of paper between the pages. They should not use anything thicker than a postcard for this purpose and they should never turn down the pages.

Parts of a book

A book consists of the following: half-title, title-page, dedication, contents, list of illustrations, introduction, preface, the text, bibliography, appendices, and index. If there is time, children should be encouraged to draw a book and roughly outline the title-page and the other parts which have been mentioned, indicating what is put on the contents page, on the list of illustrations, and in the introduction and preface. The difference between a publisher and a printer can be stated, and where to find the date of publication, a statement of the second or subsequent issues of the book, and of the note of the date of copyright which is placed on the back of the title-page for all English as well as American books. The extreme importance of the index to non-fiction books should be emphasized and the difference between an analytical index and a straightforward alphabetical one explained. Then reference books which have these different kinds of indexes should be pointed out to emphasize the importance of knowing the difference between these two kinds of index and the way in which they should be used to find the information required.

Alphabetical arrangement

Records and books in libraries are frequently kept in alphabetical order, and so that the children may understand their way about both the catalogue and also the arrangement of books on the shelves, it is desirable to explain what alphabetical order is, and the best way of doing this is not only by demonstration on a blackboard or by holding up cards, but also by making a game. Many adults have great difficulty in finding their way through an alphabetical sequence: one cannot therefore expect junior or primary school children to be able to use one without considerable practice. After writing some of the letters of the alphabet on a blackboard or holding up cards bearing these, the children can be asked to name certain objects beginning with the same letter and these are written up for everyone to see. The children are then given pieces of paper and asked to arrange the words in strict alphabetical order. When all the children have put their words into alphabetical sequence, the correct order is called out and they are asked to check their efforts with it. Their attempts at alphabetization can be examined by the teacher or librarian and any misunderstandings cleared up straight away. It is probably easier for the children to write each word on a separate piece of paper or card and to arrange the cards in order than it is to write them in correct sequence in the form of a list. When this has been done with a miscellaneous collection of words, it can be done again with a list of words beginning with another letter, or different letters, or a list of flowers, animals or towns. Finally, the children are given a set of cards on each of which has been written an author's name and they are asked to arrange these in strict order. If a dictionary catalogue is provided in the library, then cards with subjects written on them and cards with titles written on them can be interspersed with the author cards, but this should not be done until the children have arranged both subjects cards and title cards in separate groups.

Different kinds of book

The children may then be introduced to different kinds of books such as encyclopaedias, dictionaries, atlases, year-books, directories, telephone directories, etc. The purpose of each kind of book and the type of information which will be found in it should be explained at some length and the children given another game which will help them to demonstrate to the teacher or librarian whether they have grasped the difference between the various kinds of books, and make sure that they know what kind of information is to be found in them.

Encyclopaedias. Encyclopaedias are of various kinds; they are nearly always general, covering all knowledge, although some are limited to certain fields. The contributions under the different headings may vary from a very short description to an extremely long one, and if there are several encyclopaedias in the library the same heading should be looked up in each and the extent of the information in each should be indicated. It should be pointed out that encyclopaedias can be condensed into one volume or may extend to about fifty. They are usually written, not by one person, but by a number of experts in particular fields who are invited by the general editor or the board of editors to write contributions on certain subjects within their special field. Some encyclopaedias have indexes and the reason for this should be explained, especially by using the *Encyclopaedia Britannica* with its analytical index as an indication of the value of an index to a comprehensive encyclopaedia because varied information on any one subject can be found in different parts of it.

The arrangement of information in encyclopaedias such as the *Oxford junior encyclopaedia*, where an alphabetical arrangement is not followed, should be described. The children should be told to look up the names of people they are interested in under the surname, or the clan or race name, as the case may be, and to ignore both definite and indefinite articles. It should also be demonstrated to them however, if a subject is not entered under one heading, that they must think of alternative headings under which it may be entered. Some encyclopaedias use cross-references; these must be explained. After the demonstrations and explanations of the kind mentioned – and every explanation should be illustrated and emphasized by an actual demonstration of one or more encyclopaedias – the children may be given a game, or exercise, in which they are asked to look up certain information anywhere they can. If it is intended to train them to get used to the arrangement in particular books *because* of their unusual arrangement (such as the *Oxford junior encyclopaedia*), or because of the importance of the works concerned, their use of these books only would be permitted. They should be given a set of headings or subjects to look up and then write against them the page number of the book in which they have found information, or take the book to the librarian or teacher as evidence that they have found it. The latter is the better method because this will enable the instructor to help them with any little difficulties, or give them personal instruction.

If letters or words are given at the top left- or right-hand corners of pages, or in the centres of pages, or of the columns of pages, to indicate first and last entries which appear underneath, these should be explained to the children.

Dictionaries. It is important that children should be able to find their way about dictionaries easily, and this can best be taught by exercises or games following a brief description of the way the entries are arranged, and how the pages are guided by means of the inclusive words or letters which appear at the top of the pages. Exercises or games for this purpose can best be done in class where every child has an identical dictionary, but it can also be done in a children's library providing there are enough copies of the same dictionary. The intention is to drill the children to be able to find their way to required words as quickly as possible. One way is to display a list of words in front of the children, several of whom are ready as a team with their dictionaries, and at the word 'go' each picks up the book and tries to open it at approximately the right place where the word is to be found. The children are then asked what is the first word on the page where they have opened the book. If they open the book at the beginning or end, instead of in the middle, they need further training in the sequence of letters in the alphabet. Another method which can be used once they have become familiar with the sequence of letters is to write up the first and last words on two consecutive pages together with the appropriate page numbers. They are then asked on which page they will find a specific word. This will train them in the alphabetization of letters within words. They can then be asked on which of the two pages they will find several specific words, and finally, they can be asked to guess what is the last word on the page previous to the one listed and the first word on the page following the one listed.

When the children have become familiar with this aspect of the use of dictionaries, speed can be developed by getting them to take part in another game which is played as follows. Several words in different parts of the alphabet, and not in alphabetical order, are exhibited, and children who have been grouped into teams, and who have their dictionaries closed in front of them, are given a blank sheet of paper. When the signal to start is given, the first child chooses the word which is nearest to the beginning of the alphabet, consults the dictionary and enters on the paper the syllabified spelling, the correct pronunciation, and the part of speech (or such of this information as is given in the dictionary). The paper is then passed to the next child in the team who selects the next word in alphabetical order and enters the same facts as the first child did. This plan is followed until all the pupils in the team have finished, or until the signal is given to stop work. The papers are then corrected and the team with the highest score wins the game. When the children get used to playing the game in this way it can be made more effective and difficult by requiring each competitor to write a definition of the word either in his own words, or copied from the dictionary, and to illustrate its correct use in a sentence.

Another exercise in dictionary drill is to tell the children to turn to a certain page and ask them to write down a list of four or five words which the teacher mentions and to write the meanings against them. When this is done they are told to choose three words from the same page and write these down giving the meanings in the same way. Then the teacher may discuss the meanings and origin of the words and the various ways in which they can be used. Eventually, children will realize that there are five things which can be found out from a good dictionary: 1. the proper spelling of the word, 2. its correct pronunciation, 3. its meaning, 4. synonymous words, 5. the origin of the words.

Atlases. Children should be taught how to find particular maps which they require in an atlas. The contents page is essential here. They should also be shown the difference between the various kinds of maps (political, physical, population, etc.) and should have explained to them keys on each map and any other information which the particular atlas being used for demonstration can give them. The gazetteer at the end should be explained. Much of the teaching concerning the use of maps and atlases, and the information which can be found in them, is best given by the geography teacher as part of the geography course, but the librarian, whether of the children's department of a public library or of a school, should be able and prepared to give such instruction as and when required.

Yearbooks. Yearbooks are extremely important publications for giving up-to-date information of all kinds. They are general, such as *Whitaker's almanack* which gives information of all kinds relating to the whole world, but particularly to Great Britain, the *Annual register* which gives a variety of information relating to Great Britain, the *Canada yearbook* which gives information relating to Canada only, and so on. Most countries publish year books similar to the *Canada yearbook* and it is in these that the most reliable information of various kinds can be found about certain countries. The *Europa yearbook* gives a great variety of information on many aspects of national life. Each of these, or similar books, can be used in turn (but owing to the lack of duplication, by individual children only) to demonstrate the information which can be found in them. Each book should be demonstrated by screening photographs of individual pages and by displaying the more important ones at some length, and the children should be given exercises or games in which they are asked to find specific information, which is copied out by them, from each of the books. It is essential in describing each book to go over the contents page, to indicate the arrangement of the information, and to emphasize that in many cases it is absolutely necessary to use the index. In some cases these indexes are not straightforward alphabetical ones but are subject indexes, various aspects of a subject being entered in alphabetical order under the subject name. It is important to phrase the questions in such an exercise or game simply and in such a way that children can go to the right part of the book and find the specific information required without being confused. It should be pointed out that the information in these books is always more recent than that in encyclopaedias which are only revised every few years, except in the case of the *Encyclopaedia Britannica* and *Chambers' encyclopaedia* which are constantly undergoing partial revision.

Publications such as *Keesing's contemporary archives* should then be explained, for this contains information relating to happenings all over the world and is a most important source book. It should be emphasized that in this book the information is provided on loose sheets which are received regularly by subscribers and which have to be inserted in the binders provided. The indexes and the cumulative indexes should be explained. Similar publications are *African recorder* and *Asian recorder*. The last relates almost exclusively to India, although there is some coverage of non-Indian Asian periodicals and newspapers.

Note making

This is largely a matter for teachers rather than librarians, but the teacher-librarians and librarians of children's departments of public libraries should be aware of the best way in which notes should be taken so that when the need arises they can advise the children. Before children have to take extensive notes they should have learned to read sufficiently well to understand the passage or chapter to be read. They should then be shown by demonstration the most important and relative information to their need in what they are reading, and they should be given specific practice in summarizing and condensing the information and arranging it under sub-headings if this is desirable. It is absolutely essential to discourage children from merely copying passages from books into their notebooks and so into essays. They should be taught to make notes as briefly as possible and it should be emphasized that these notes are merely mental reminders of what they have learned. One has seen children spending hours in the library copying pages of notes word by word into their exercise books. These are then served up in their essays or exercises and the children are only able to repeat what they have read; they do not thoroughly learn and understand it. The result is that although they can answer a question if it is given in exactly the same form as in the book they have read, when they are asked the same question in a different form they are completely at a loss. This has very serious repercussions when they have left school and started studying for professional examinations. Proper note-taking is largely a question of constant guidance from teachers, and insistence that the children take notes which are really brief and not copied extracts from what they have read, and that they summarize the information in their own words.

Whenever they take notes the children should get into the habit of writing the source of the information i.e., the author and title of the book and the class number if it is one in the library. Should they wish to refer again to the book, especially a week or so afterwards, they are then able to go back to the correct book without any difficulty. When about to take notes they should read the passage a second time to make sure that they thoroughly understand it. The dictionary should be consulted for meanings of new words. When they feel they understand the passage sufficiently to reproduce it in their own words, possibly using headings and sub-headings, they can then begin their notes; they should also be taught how to make abbreviations of words and to omit unessential words. When the notes are finished they should be looked through thoughtfully so that the children understand mentally what the notes are intended to convey and should then write them up in the essay, or exercise, or whatever it may be, in good English, keeping the source books closed.

Introducing the children to the library

When children are first introduced to the library, whether as members who wish to borrow books for home reading, or as students to undertake private reading or study in the library, they should first of all (if they are a group) be given a short talk on the arrangement of the books in which it is explained that the story books are arranged alphabetically by authors' names and non-fiction books by subject, that numbers on the backs of the books represent subjects, and that within each subject group the books are arranged in alphabetical order. This leads to a brief outline of the scheme of classification indicating how to use an index to the classification to find subjects. An explanation of the catalogue naturally follows a description of the classification. The main arrangement of the catalogue should be explained, and it should also be emphasized that whereas the classification is a means for arranging books by the same or related subjects at the same or near-by positions on the shelves, the catalogue is a record of the books which are in the stock of the library.

The children should also be given brief information concerning the rules of behaviour in the library and for the issue of books. An indication of the facilities available would follow. If the children are in groups, and notes can be made, so much the better. The children are then taken round the shelves in small groups of not more than about eight or ten and the theory which has been explained to them is then demonstrated in practice at the shelves and at the catalogue. The aim of the librarian should be to provide an opportunity for giving the children such information as will help them find books they need, and also, as they make use of the library afterwards, to assist in maintaining order and help to keep books in their proper places. If there is no printed schedule of the classification available for the children to consult it is a good plan to have either a film strip, or some slides, or even a chart showing the main classes of the classification and how these are sub-divided. It is also desirable to describe and illustrate the catalogue in the same way, showing cards for author, title and subject entries. When the children have been shown how to find books on particular subjects or to find entries in the catalogue under authors' names, titles or subjects, this knowledge can be further emphasized by giving them particulars of books or information to find in the library. The children can be given slips of paper asking them to find books on certain subjects (known to be on the shelves) and also entries in the catalogue for books on particular subjects or by particular authors. Although it is a general principal when classifying a book to put the book at the most specific place which can be found in the schedules, for example, books on electrical engineering would be under 'Engineering, electrical' and not under 'Engineering', it is essential to point out to the children that if they cannot find a subject heading in the catalogue, or the index to the classification, or the index to the catalogue (according to the kind of catalogue in use), they should look under an alternative. In any case they should think of alternative titles, for the classifier and cataloguer may, for example, have thought of indexing a book on radio under 'wireless' and not under 'radio', and although it is desirable in such cases to put entries under synonymous headings in the index one cannot expect every cataloguer to think of all alternative headings, neither can one expect the cataloguer to know all the synonymous headings for subjects which are not of general interest.

Reading for pleasure

One of the chief aims of the librarian, whether of a school library or of a children's department of a public library, is to encourage the children to get into the habit of reading for pleasure as well as for information. In modern life there are many things to distract people, and especially children, from reading books; it has been alleged but without very much foundation, that the introduction of radio and television caused a temporary reduction in the reading of books. There was a slight reduction which *could* be traced to television very soon after it was introduced, but this only lasted for a short time. There is now much purposeful reading actually inspired by television and it is generally accepted that radio and television have the effect of increasing rather than decreasing the use of books. Many librarians take advantage of broadcast and televised programmes to introduce to children books which otherwise they would not see, or might overlook. This can be done by publishing duplicated or printed lists of books, but more effectively by arranging displays of books in the library with a subject heading very closely allied to the title of the series of talks, etc., which are broadcast or televised.

The children's librarian has also to combat the prevalence of poorer quality literature in the form of badly written and badly produced periodicals and comics; although much of this material is exciting and attractive to children, it is often badly written, and the best way of leading children away from this is constantly to bring to their attention books and periodicals of better quality. There must of course be an adequate supply of such publications, and titles should be duplicated to such an extent that one can always expect to find at least one copy on the shelves. These books should be attractive in appearance in addition to being well written. Children's librarians need to know the types of stories that children like to read, and must select books for the library to satisfy their interests.

Apart from enquiring personally of children and thereby getting to know at first hand their favourite kinds of book or author, there are other ways in which this information can be obtained, and several teachers, educationists and librarians have conducted enquiries into children's reading tastes. The results should always be considered carefully in relation to the age range of the children because children's tastes, and also their favourite authors, differ considerably according to their age. If children who are members of a library are asked to fill up a questionnaire, such a questionnaire should always require them to state their age. Teachers have a very much better opportunity than children's librarians of guiding children's reading and forming good literary taste, but the methods which they use can also be used to some extent by the librarians of children's departments of public libraries. One extremely good method is to read to groups of children extracts from a book which is considered worth recommending and to stop reading at an exciting passage. The children can then be invited to put their names down on a list to read the book. It must, however, first of all be ascertained that there are enough copies to meet the demand which is likely to arise without the children having to wait too long for the book.

Other methods which have been used with considerable success are to let the children contribute book reviews to a periodical publication issued by the library, or for exhibition in the class-room or library. Another method is to invite the children to address the other members of a library 'club' or reading group, telling them of the books they have read and why they enjoyed them. Interest can also be aroused in the work of a particular author by getting the children to look up particulars concerning him and to obtain copies of his books, biographies, photographs of him at work and in his home, reviews of books written, and articles about him culled from periodicals, and so on.

The teacher concerned with this subject will want to know what the children are reading so as to find out their reactions to a certain book, or to certain kinds of books, to know whether they are reading the books which they are being encouraged to read, and to know that they really are reading them and not just reporting that they have done so.

CO-OPERATION BETWEEN SCHOOL LIBRARY AND PUBLIC LIBRARY

Before co-operation between school and public library is considered, it may be as well briefly to consider the functions of both these kinds of library.

The function of the school library
Every school needs a library of its own to make the work of the school more truly effective and also to develop in the pupils the habit of using books in connection with their

school interests, with their learning, with their hobbies and with their out-of-school interests. A school caters exclusively for its own pupils and their educational needs, and its library is geared to provide books which can be used to supplement classroom studies. In a secondary school there is need for a large collection of reference books (i.e. dictionaries, gazetteers, year books, encyclopaedias and other books in which the information is provided in such a way that the books would not be read through) as well as other books, which the pupils will use to assist them with their homework and to supplement classroom instruction.

There is a place for fiction in every school library but as it is not necessary to provide a complete range of children's fiction suitable for the children attending the school, it need only be sufficient to whet the children's appetite for leisure reading and to supplement and illustrate English, geography or history lessons.

The above are minimum provisions. Where there is no public library service within easy access of a school, then the function of the school library needs to be widened so as to provide the facilities normally available at public libraries.

The proximity, or otherwise, of a public library will also affect a decision as to whether or not the school library should lend books for home-reading. If children are to be encouraged to develop the reading habit, and there is no well-stocked public library which the children can use, then obviously the school library must not be merely a reference library, or one from which books may only be borrowed for use in class, but must provide books for home reading as well. To do this properly will not only cost much more money for books and stationery, but more assistants (including possibly a full-time qualified librarian) will be needed.

The function of a public library

The function of a children's department of a public library

is to perform the same services as the school library, but to do so for all the children in the community. The children's department of a public library provides books for all children – for the pre-school child right through to the fourteen- or fifteen-year-old. The number of books is normally very much greater, and the range and choice much wider than is normally found in most schools, and there is often very much more duplication of titles than is possible in schools. This is largely due to the public library having more money for books than schools, which often have to raise money by holding concerts or draw on a small fund which is provided for a variety of functions. It is also due to more librarians in public libraries being trained in library work. The public library provides for the varied interests of all children and sets out to encourage children to develop the profitable use of leisure by creating the habit of reading. Once an adequate quantity of suitable books has been provided, there is little difficulty in developing this habit, for normal children who have learned to read easily soon become avid readers. The public library is free to everybody and there is normally no restraint, and very few restrictions, on its use; members have the advantage of complete freedom of action within the regulations. If a child does not want to read, he need not; and he feels no compunction once he is in the library, to read anything which is there if he does not want to. In a school library there may sometimes be pressure, or the children may *feel* there is pressure on them, to read when they are disinclined to do so, or to read certain books.

Co-operation between school and public library is very largely one-sided. This is inevitable because public libraries have, generally speaking, been in operation longer than school libraries; they are often larger, and they are administered by professional librarians.

One of the most important means of co-operation is for

the public library to make the children's library, and also
the books, available to classes of children who can attend
during school time for project work. If the children's library
is too small to accommodate a full class of children, and it is
considered worth while allowing the children to use the
public library books, then it may be possible for books to be
lent to the school for a definite period of, say, a month or a
term (providing the stock of books is adequate for this
purpose).

Loans of books to schools
A school library's stock of books should be sufficient to
meet normal needs, but sometimes when special projects
are being worked on, or unusual subjects are being taught, it
is necessary to supplement the school library's normal stock
with other books, and these can sometimes be borrowed
from the children's department of the local public library.
Where schools suffer from a severe limitation of funds for
library purposes it would be uneconomic to spend such
funds on books not likely to be in constant use. This difficulty
does not arise so much in the public library because the
demand is more constant and comes from a very much
greater clientele. Loans to the school from a larger collection
such as that of the public library, or from a headquarters
if the various school libraries in the district are under one
control, is more satisfactory than the schools adding to
their permanent stock books likely to be in demand only
occasionally. Also the lending of such books from the
public library benefits the public library too, because the
children will know that the books have come from the
public library and it will thereby be brought to the notice
of the children, who, if interested, may go there for further
books.

Bulk loans of this nature cannot be made by the public
library if its own stock is not large, and if the making of such

loans would reduce the number of books available to members to such an extent that the choice left on the shelves would be considerably impoverished. It would be foolish for the public library to reduce its own resources by lending books in bulk to schools when the schools should themselves have adequate funds to provide the books which they really need. If such conditions exist it is better for the children to attend the public library in school time to use the books there and to borrow books for reading at home.

There are, however, circumstances which make it desirable, even if the users of a public library may suffer to some extent, to lend books in bulk to the school library. For instance, when children have difficulty in using the public library, either because of inadequate travel facilities, or the fact that they have to leave school by school 'bus in order to reach their homes which may be several miles away, or where a school library has been established so short a time that it has not been able to accumulate an adequate stock. Other reasons which justify bulk loans from public libraries to school libraries are (a) the children may be too small to be able to travel to a distant public library; (b) the parents, or even the teachers, may be reluctant to allow the children to use the public library for some reason; (c) the children may be physically handicapped. If teachers are likely to need bulk loans for a fairly long period, say a term, it is an advantage if they can let the public librarian know several weeks in advance which books they will require, or on which subjects they will require books, in order that he may check his resources, and if necessary buy additional books. These special purchases would not be looked upon as being made specially for the school as the books would go into the ordinary stock of the library when the school had finished with them. Such requests would probably reveal gaps in the stock of the library of which the librarian might not be aware.

Assistance for the school librarian

The librarian of the children's department of a public library can often give the school librarian considerable assistance in the matter of book selection. It is the children's librarian's job to know books; she is constantly discovering new books, she gets to know the contents of books on certain subjects, and sub-consciously builds up an evaluative knowledge of children's books which may be much greater than that of the average teacher or school librarian. She is also more familiar with new publications, both books and periodicals. If good relationships have been established between school and children's librarians, the school librarian can often tap the knowledge and resources of children's librarians without embarrassment. She may also allow a school teacher or teacher-librarian to look through her recent additions to stock. This may give the teacher-librarian an idea of books which would be suitable to add to her own stock.

Nearly all public libraries now have trained children's librarians at work in their children's departments; their training will have been received by working under supervision in a children's library and attending lectures in children's literature and the techniques of running children's libraries, and by attendance at special courses. Their technical knowledge will include not only an ability to select, catalogue and classify books, but also other matters such as library planning and furnishing, methods of displaying periodicals and books, extension work, and the many routines connected with running this department. Here again if good relationships have been built up between the school librarian and the children's librarian, this knowledge will be imparted quite readily.

Additional tickets for teachers. It makes for good school and library relations, and also assists the teachers in their work, if they can be given additional tickets to enable them to borrow either children's books or books from the adult department which they need in connection with their school work.

Teachers probably require books for their work much more than any other group of people and there should never therefore be any hesitation in allowing them to have additional books. The whole tenor of the public library service today is to make it possible to meet readers' needs, and regulations are sometimes interpreted flexibly to make this possible.

In some countries it is necessary to guard against the transfer of members' tickets from one person to another, and also against the use of tickets for purposes other than those for which they were issued; local conditions must always determine action.

Assistance for the children's librarian

The assistance which the school librarian can give the children's librarian of a public library is very largely informal and individual. Teachers can help in building up a story hour or a lecture programme, and are often willing to take part in such activities themselves. They will also be willing to give assistance in running book discussion or play reading groups, or in making puppets as a library activity, and the giving of puppet shows. They can also quite often advise the children's librarian on books on specific subjects.

Teachers can directly assist the work of the children's library by distributing tickets for talks and film shows, by displaying jackets of books added to the public library, and by exhibiting or distributing lists of books and any printed or duplicated bulletins which the library may issue. They can talk about the books, especially the new ones in the public library, and use them in class; by so doing a taste for literature is being inculcated and the habit of reading for pleasure formed. If the teacher looks upon the public library as a supplement to the school's resources, and uses it considerably herself, the children will eventually realise that the public library is a place to which they can go for books for themselves.

Teachers can help the public library by signing recommendations for the children to become members. They can assist in endeavouring to secure the return of books which children have borrowed from the public library and kept longer than they should have done. Children's librarians often hesitate to approach teachers in this matter, but there is no reason why they should hesitate if the teachers look upon the public library, as they should (and mostly do), as an important asset to the children's educational, cultural and social development.

One of the ways in which the teacher can introduce the children to the library is to take them in a class and let the children's librarian talk to them about the books, the way they are arranged, and the facilities available. The children will then probably want to join the library and become borrowers.

When children begin a project in a public library it is a good idea for the children's librarian to give them an introductory talk on reference books and the information that can be found in them, and also on the catalogue, the classification, the way the books are arranged, and so on. This talk is even more valuable if the children's librarian turns it into a competitive game, handing out slips with items and information written on them which the children are asked to find in certain books and then show to either the children's librarian or the teacher for verification.

It will be seen from the foregoing that close and harmonious co-operation between school and children's librarians will result in furthering the effectiveness of their respective libraries. To summarize, teachers need to know the value of books, to know the contents of books, and to know how the public library can help both themselves and the children. They will need to know the conditions under which the children may join the library, including age limits if there are any, and the number of tickets available to the children. The children's librarian needs to know the teacher's aims, his ideals, and his book problems. If teacher and children's librarian visit one another in their respective places of employment for an informal chat, or for formal business such as a talk by the children's librarian to a class of children or by a teacher taking a class to visit the library, they will both begin to understand how they can help one another. Very often this help need not be formal; informal help may be all that is required, but providing this friendship and awareness of one another's needs and problems has been established then friendly and beneficial co-operation will result.

The librarian will find the teacher can give her very much assistance, especially if she is new to the district, or if a children's library service is being established for the first time, for the teacher will be able to tell her something about the district, about the children, their background, their home life, their habits and their interests. All this is very useful to the children's librarian in her approach to her job, for it helps her to anticipate problems which may arise in dealing with the children and to assess, even if vaguely, their potential reading abilities.

Unified control
It will be realised that co-operation between school and public librarian depends very largely on personalities, on a willingness to meet the other half way, and on understanding the others' aims and functions.

Co-operation will not always work. Sometimes there is antipathy which has existed for many years between school and library. This may have been engendered at the top, for example between the education officer and the chief librarian. Although in these days this seldom happens, if it does exist it is likely to permeate eventually to the youngest library assistant and teacher. The latter, however, can, if they have a mind to, do much to improve relations at the lowest level. If there are basic objections to co-operation in a particular place, it will probably be better in the interests of the children and their future use of a public library service if school and public libraries could be placed under one control – that of the public librarian. Quite often school libraries and public libraries receive their finances from the same basic source, and for this reason there would seem to be no very great obstacle to single control. Objections would probably come from head teachers of schools who would feel that something which they should be doing was being done by the public librarian, for obviously if there were one control of the libraries it would have to be by the professional librarian as the most experienced and best-informed person to run libraries of any kind. These two services could be provided as separate branches of one organization, or they could be two separately financed services (schools and public libraries) under one administration, the school library service being paid for by a different authority, or fund, to the public library service, but administered by the public librarian as agent.

There are economic advantages of administration under one control; books can be bought by one person, or one team, with smaller administrative overhead charges than by two. The larger the number of schools in an area, the smaller in relationship to the number of books bought would these charges become. There are also indirect economic advantages in that the public library with the larger resources that a group of libraries in one organization can provide and a headquarters reserve of books, supplemented by the combined stocks of several schools, could co-ordinate the work of all the service points and arrange for books to be sent to any school or library when requested.

Libraries during the past twenty years have developed co-operation in book loans to a very marked degree, and there is no reason why co-ordinated school and public libraries should not work quite satisfactorily under one administration. Overall standards of efficiency would be ensured by having two or three highly qualified and experienced children's librarians at the head of the service; this would result in the advantages (but not the disadvantages) of standardization, in that classification, cataloguing, the keeping of various records, and so on, would be similar. There would also be economies in the cost of binding books, and in the avoidance of unnecessary duplication in the purchase of books. There is little doubt that the standard of provision in school libraries would be very much higher than if the school libraries were left to the teachers who might not be particularly interested or experienced, and might not know the best books.

There might be objections by the teachers to a co-ordinated service of this kind on the grounds that the school libraries were being provided and imposed from above by people not familiar with the needs of the children, etc. This could easily be overcome or avoided by having a joint committee of an equal number of school librarians or head teachers and of children's librarians in the public libraries under the chairmanship of the chief librarian. This committee could consider such policy matters as the standard of provision, the number of books to be made available in various schools, and the type of books needed.

School libraries should *belong* to the school and this could be quite easily arranged in a co-ordinated service, especially if the books in the school and public libraries were provided from common funds. If the basis of provision were the expenditure of a fixed sum per pupil there could be no question as to some schools being better treated than others. Individual teachers or teacher-librarians would have opportunities of requesting that specific books should be added to their libraries and these requests would, within reason, be granted. The school library should be considered to *belong* to the school because it is an integral part of the school's provision and equipment, and an essential part of the teaching facilities. Who finances or administers the library should make no difference to its status.

CHAPTER III

The Physical Library

THE BUILDING AND ITS EQUIPMENT

In an urban area

There are many factors which determine whether a separate building shall be provided for a library, whether it should be large or small, or of a temporary or permanent nature. Factors which determine the situation and kind of building which should be provided are: (a) the climate; (b) public transport; (c) the extent of literacy in the area; (d) the density of the population. These factors also influence the provision of a library for adults as well as for children.

To take these one by one, climatic conditions will influence the willingness of people to visit the library, e.g. in tropical countries people tend to avoid going out in the heat of the sun as much as possible, and therefore they make use of public amenities, go visiting, exercise and entertain themselves when the sun is losing its intensity. In some countries rainy seasons may be such that people are almost housebound for long periods. These conditions can have a considerable influence on the use of a library. The climate of a temperate zone does not have such an influence on people's movements.

With regard to public transport, this is probably the biggest factor influencing the use of a library. Whether residents rely very largely on public transport or have their own transport, a library should be sited in a shopping area especially if at the junction of cross roads or on bus routes. If a library can be provided in such a situation, its use will be assured, providing that the first and most important requirement in any library – a good book stock – is satisfied. If public transport communications are good these will counteract to some extent any effect which the climate may have. In towns where a high proportion of the residents own motor-cars, the bus routes are not such important factors. One cannot go far wrong if the library is placed near the post office for this is usually in the centre of the shopping area.

The extent of literacy in the area will also affect the use of any books which are provided, and consequently the size of the library building and the extent and range of its book stock. In a district where people have become literate only recently there is more need for periodicals than for books, and consequently for reading-rooms rather than lending libraries. Literacy also determines the proportion of adult books to children's books and also of simple children's books compared with those intended for older children.

The density of the population considerably influences the size of the library and the type of provision most needed. For example, in a thinly populated district there will be more demand for lending library than for reference library facilities, and it may not be necessary to provide more than a very few general reference books.

In a densely populated part of London, with excellent train and 'bus communications, a survey showed that people would not travel more than just over half a mile to a library. In such a case it is therefore desirable to place library buildings at intervals of slightly more than a mile apart.

One should avoid placing children's libraries in positions where children will have to contend with traffic hazards. If it is at all possible, they should not be sited on main roads but if this is inevitable, or for other reasons desirable, the entrance should be in a side road. On the other hand, important traffic focal points, where several busy roads converge, are the most suitable places for a library from the point of view of convenience to the public. In a thickly populated urban area bisected by extremely busy main roads, the best way to provide children's library services and at the same time avoid traffic hazards, is to place libraries in each of the community areas formed by the main roads.

Also, if at all possible, the libraries for children should be placed near a group of schools, or within easy reach of them. The children will then find it convenient to visit the library on their way to or from school. In any case children should not be expected to travel long distances.

Where there is a very large child population, or where very few adults are literate but the children are able to read, libraries are sometimes provided for children only.

Usually in urban areas a children's library, or at any rate a collection of children's books, is provided at every library service point.

The kinds of service provided in the library depend very largely on the type of district. If a branch library is in a recently developed residential district, one can anticipate that a much larger proportion of the people living there will be children, and consequently there will be a greater need for children's books. If, on the other hand, the branch library is in a predominantly commercial or industrial district where the children are mainly those of caretakers or persons who must live near the places of business because of the nature of their work, then the number of children's books must obviously be very much smaller. If there are several schools in the district, as there may well be in some cities, even in districts which are not predominantly residential, then a larger portion of the library building must be allocated for the use of children; in fact quite a large proportion may be necessary because large numbers of children will use it during their lunch-hour or immediately after school. At other times, unless many children live near, the children's library may be almost empty except for classes doing project work with their teachers during school time. Children's libraries in districts which are not residential, or where there are no schools nearby, are used hardly at all.

In a rural area

The problem of providing a children's library in a rural district is often greater than in an urban area because it is not so easy to find a site which is equally convenient to all the residents. If there is a village centre or a community centre, or if the shops or schools are close together, then any of these places is suitable for a children's library. Sometimes resort has to be made to sharing other public buildings such as a clinic or a post office – or a shop may have to be rented.

If a rural area has no natural centre of this kind it is probably better not to provide a static library service, for the population is likely to be too small to justify the capital expenditure involved in keeping a collection of books there; in such circumstances it is better to have a mobile library visit the school and also parts of the area for short intervals, say of an hour or so, every week. The school children can borrow books when it visits the school, and younger children when it goes to the other 'stands'. The overheads involved in providing a static library are almost certain not to be justified in such an area. A static library should only be provided if it is likely to be in full use twenty hours a week, even if this means that the public do not have access to the wider services that such a library provides.

When should separate accommodation for children be provided?

In a residential district where there is a large child population, as in housing development areas containing large numbers of flats, where these flats are allocated on the basis of the number of children in the family (the larger families having higher priorities), it may be advisable to have a separate building for children only, rather than to provide accommodation in a branch library. This is particularly desirable when there are traffic hazards, such as very busy main roads or road junctions, in the district. Such a library was provided in Islington just after the last war when an area near King's Cross Station was being rebuilt after severe damage by enemy bombs, and several blocks of flats were erected. It was not necessary to make provision for adults as there was a branch library little more than a half mile away, but there was a long and very busy main road leading from the area mentioned to it. The building, which was erected as part of the estate, fully justified the expense, and this building, although not large (it shelves about 2,000 volumes), immediately became – and has remained – popular.

Where potential usage of the library is not large enough to justify a separate building for children, but the branch library has a total accommodation for approximately 5,000 books, a separate room for the use of the children would be justified. Whenever the use of the library is large enough to warrant a separate room, this should be provided because children have a sense of proprietorship and pride in a room which is set aside for them; and it is therefore something which they can be encouraged to regard as their own. They will take an interest not only in using it but also in running it. A separate room can be made very much more a unit than if the children's portion of a library is merely a part, or a corner, of another room.

Where the use of a branch library is not large enough to justify a separate room, a portion of the adult library is usually reserved exclusively for the use of the children. The furniture of the one-room library should be designed as a whole, the shelves for the children's books being the same height as for the adults', but the top shelf can be filled in with a framework covered with cork to serve as a place on which to pin tier guides or paper cut-outs; if it is hinged at the top it can also serve as a cupboard for reserved books, those requiring re-binding, posters, etc. The children's portion should have smaller tables and chairs than the standard size, and shelves for reference books should be provided.

If a separate room is provided for boys and girls it should be close to, and if possible adjoining, the adult library. This has the advantage that the children, when using it, see their parents and other adults using the adult library and they realize that their department is part of a bigger organization. When they feel they have no more use for the junior library but are ready to read books in the adult library, it will be an easy and natural progression from one department to the other.

For the same reason it is desirable that there should not be a separate entrance to the children's library unless the main entrance to the building is on a busy street with a traffic hazard; a less dangerous entrance can then be provided on a side street.

If the Browne method of recording loans is used in the children's library and an entirely different, mechanized, system is used for adults' books, this complicates the use of one enclosure for both groups of readers. It is then better to deal with loans to children in the children's library.

One staff enclosure serving both the adult and the children's departments also helps the children realize that they are part of a larger organization; there is the added advantage from the staffing point of view in that the same staff discharging or issuing adult books can also deal with children's books. There are, however, two disadvantages: one is that the staff attending to children (and who should be allocated to the children's library so that they can specialize in this branch of library work to some extent) do not get to

know the children by name or the type of books that individual children usually borrow. This is desirable for reading
guidance and for good borrower/staff relationships. The
second disadvantage is that when the library is busy at rush
periods with large numbers of children, they tend to block
the entrance of the staff enclosure to the inconvenience and
sometimes the annoyance of adult members. This difficulty
can be avoided by having a small separate counter built for
the discharging of children's books. Books for children and
adults are discharged at one side of the staff enclosure,
except when the library is busy, as is usual after afternoon
school, and on Saturdays. The trays containing the charges of
books issued to children, which are filed separately from
those issued to adults, should then be taken from the main
staff enclosure to the smaller counter, which may be placed
to form a passage alongside the enclosure of approximately
2 feet 3 inches wide. The bolts securing this counter to the
floor can be withdrawn and the counter, which should be on
castors, moved away, thus doubling in width the entrance
to the library. The children can be attended to at this small
counter while adults are attended to immediately behind
them in another parallel queue by staff in the main staff
enclosure. As the issue of books is a much quicker function
that the discharging of books, except where charging is
done by micro-photography, all the books should be issued
at the exit side of the main staff enclosure.

Such arrangements as these can be made even if the
children's library is in a separate department.

Another criterion for deciding on a separate entrance
could be usage: a thousand loans for home reading a week
justifies a separate entrance.

Where children's libraries are in separate buildings from
the adult libraries, and the children consequently never see
the adults when using their own libraries, there is a risk that
they will grow into adolescence without being aware of the

adult library – unless of course their parents are members.

Stairs should not lead to the children's library because of the temptation this offers for play.

Neither should this department be in a basement or semi-basement. Children may get the impression (unless there is a separate entrance at a lower level than the main entrance) that they are inferior. Rooms in these positions require more artificial light if natural lighting is not good, and they may also be difficult to ventilate. They need more supervision and are less likely to be seen and used by adults on behalf of children. Windows at or below street level provide problems of discipline and also of cleaning.

Physical conditions

There are three physical conditions which must be considered in connexion with the children's library as with any other department. These are lighting, heating and ventilation; whatever the climatic conditions, each can affect the comfort of the readers.

Dust, damp, heat, and in some countries insects and termites, are the chief sources of damage to books (apart from the ravages of very small children and puppies) and these potential risks can be greatly reduced by appropriate building design and good, sound construction. Dust is a problem in most libraries and often cannot be prevented, only reduced by not being allowed to accumulate. Damp is reducible by air control by means of windows, heating or air conditioning. Heat damage is caused by permitting the sun's rays to reach the books, or by not protecting the books placed near heating elements. Insects can be destroyed by painting suitable liquids on shelves, mixing DDT with paint or puffing insect-killing powders on to the shelves and the books, and painting a suitable solution on the joints of the bindings. The problem of termites is one for the architect when drawing up the specification for the building.

Lighting and ventilation. Windows should be as high as possible, for a window at the top of the wall gives much more light than one of the same size lower down. For this reason horizontal windows are preferable to perpendicular ones. They also permit, even in modern low-ceilinged rooms, book cases to be placed against the walls. Windows which allow the sun's rays to penetrate at a low angle should be avoided if possible; otherwise they should be screened or the light softened by using curtains or blinds. Contemporary architectural styles provide some measure of shading by building louvres at right angles to the windows, either perpendicularly or horizontally, to reduce the length of time which the sun's rays penetrate a room. It may seem unreasonable to keep the sun out of a room, but although the sun has many benefits, its rays are damaging to plastic sleeves on books, bindings, fabrics and furniture, and are uncomfortable for staff and readers who have to sit in it for a long time. If shades or curtains are to be used, proper provision for fixing these should be made during the construction of the building.

Facilities for closing windows quickly are essential, preferably in groups and not individually, by electrical or mechanical means. The cleaning of windows can be a problem unless they have been designed so that this can be carried out easily.

In tropical and semi-tropical countries, prevailing winds (or the absence of winds) and monsoons bring their problems. Usually it is necessary to provide the maximum of direct cross ventilation and at the same time keep out driving rain. This last can be accomplished by having the equivalent of a balcony outside the library walls with open windows or window spaces, by building wide overhanging eaves, or by building a grille some two feet or so from the walls.

As an alternative to direct and cross ventilation, or to supplement this, large-bladed fans may be fixed to revolve about three feet below a high ceiling; these cause movement of the air but do not fully circulate it, and help to make rooms bearable.

Where air-conditioning is provided, none of these afore-mentioned problems (and others caused by climatic condi-tions) arise, providing it is of the kind which draws air into the building, de-humidifies and cleans it, and either warms or cools it as may be necessary. But one may then have the problems from time to time of the plant being out of action for maintenance, or because of broken 'parts', or the failure of electricity supplies. At these times the buildings are almost unusable except at great personal discomfort.

Roof lighting should never be provided in any building. Overhead sunlight penetration is a disadvantage in any climate and one cannot be certain that roof lights are going to be permanently watertight.

The use of light-reflecting materials such as hard plastic wall coverings or glass tiles, and of glass bricks to admit light, add considerably to the brightness of the interiors of buildings.

Artificial lighting is another matter which has to be given consideration quite early on in the planning of a children's library. The lighting standard should be good; it is measured in terms of 'lumens per foot' (formerly 'foot-candles'), one lumen being the strength of the light of one candle measured one foot from the light source. The American lighting engineers have higher standards in this matter than the British, and recommend eighty lumens for a library.

The best form of lighting is general lighting (i.e. light values being the same throughout a room), the light source being in troughs embedded in the ceiling. This is a 'direct' method of lighting, all the light rays being thrown down. If this is structurally impossible (and this is often the case except when provision is made during the construction of the building) then fittings can be used which throw all the light

downwards. This is not however aesthetically very satisfactory and it is better to have 'semi-direct' or 'semi-indirect'
fittings which are designed to throw varying proportions –
a third or more – of the light rays to the ceiling and walls
(which must be of a light colour) whence they are reflected.
Suspended fittings are best avoided if possible for they are a
source of dust accumulation, and need cleaning – this is
sometimes difficult to carry out. Moreover they are often
'stylist', ugly and obtrusive. A person should not be aware
when entering a room of an obtrusive source of artificial
light.

Point lighting (the fitting of light fittings to tables and
bookcases) should under no circumstances be permitted for
the following reasons: (a) the fittings are often obtrusive;
(b) they cause a contrast of light intensity between the area
specifically illuminated and surrounding areas, and this
causes a certain amount of strain on the eyes; (c) they cause
reflection of light from the pages of open books or table tops
and this is also a strain on the eyes; (d) lower shelves of cases
which have lights fitted to them are inadequately lighted
while the upper shelves are lighted excessively; (e) furniture
to which fittings are secured cannot be moved except at the
considerable expense of re-wiring and possibly supplying
new fittings.

The colours that are used on ceilings and walls have a
great effect on the lighting of rooms. For this reason only
light colours with a high reflection value should be used. Any
desire on the part of architect or interior decorator to use a
currently fashionable colour scheme which is contrary to
this principle should be strongly resisted. I am familiar with
a college library which has a tile-red ceiling (the only
room in the building with so dark a colour!), and although
white opaque light fittings – the best form of semi-indirect
light fitting – are used, the effectiveness of the lighting is
reduced to an inadequate standard, despite the use of bulbs

of high wattage. In addition, the consumption of electricity is greatly, and unnecessarily (but compulsorily) increased.

A. H. Munsell (1858–1915), a Boston art teacher, produced his first colour chart in 1905, and from this, the important and internationally recognised Munsell Colour Reference System has developed. This records the reflection values of the five principal hues (yellow, green, blue, purple and red) and of the five intermediate hues (green yellow, blue green, purple blue, red purple and yellow red). Generally speaking, the lightest shades of these colours (except of green, blue green and purple blue) which have an approximate reflection of 60% or more are suitable for use on walls and ceilings where the reflection of light is desirable. The Building Bulletin No. 9 *Colour in school buildings*, published by the Department of Education and Science, describes this system briefly, includes 47 colours in the Archrome (Munsell) Range on a colour card and gives the relevant reflection data. It also offers very useful suggestions for the use of colours in particular situations and gives information about different paint finishes.

Heating. The children's library should be comfortably warm, never getting below 18°C (65°F) which is considered in Europe to be a reasonable indoor temperature. It is also the best temperature in which to keep books. In tropical and semi-tropical countries it is sometimes not possible to reduce the temperature below about 24°C (75°F) even with air-conditioning. A problem in some countries in the so-called temperate zones is to keep out cold winds and draughts. This is best done by means of double-glazing which should consist of either removable glazed screens or draught-proof double windows so made that when the weather is not cold the windows can be opened for ventilation. Where this cannot be afforded the effect of cold wind penetration can be reduced by hanging thick curtains at the windows. When the cost of these, and their fitting, cleaning and renewal over the years, is taken into account, there can be very little difference in the cost of both methods.

The design of the building can help in respect of cold winds. The door to the children's library should not open off a cold and draughty hall or staircase, neither should it open directly on to the street, without some protection such as a porch and two sets of doors. One such building was so cold that glazed screens had to be erected to protect the children and the staff from the full effect of the north winds – but the winds were only funnelled to other parts of the library; they were not kept out. They could so easily have been if a porch had been built to protect the entrance and two sets of doors provided. A revolving door is useful in this connexion; but it is a temptation to children to push it round several times and then let it spin with the momentum caused. Two sets of doors are better.

The kind of heating provided depends largely on what is generally available in the country. The circulation of hot water through a building seems to be as satisfactory as any, and the type of fitting which obscures the dust-collecting ribs of radiators has greatly improved the appearance of this kind of fitting. In recent years there has been a return to the Roman system of heated air which enters the rooms from louvres in the trunking, and it has gained favour.

Electricity is only suitable in countries where the cost of production is exceptionally low. Under-floor heating, whether electricity or hot water, is expensive to instal and run, and also has the disadvantage of being uncomfortable for those who have to 'be on their feet' for a long time. A night-storage installation provides reduced charges and may be cheaper except in severe weather when boosting is necessary. In public buildings where exterior doors are constantly being opened, and sometimes left open unintentionally, heat loss is considerable, and any boosting of the temperature which has to be done before the current automatically comes on in the

evening is exceptionally expensive. Where there is a very
heavy consumption load in excessively cold weather, due to
the demands of industry, supplies may be cut off temporarily.
Electric wall panel heaters should not be used higher than
waist level, neither should they be used where the surrounding wall is likely to become blackened.

Whatever form of heating is provided, its controls should
not be placed within children's reach, and thermostats
should be fitted in every room so that a predetermined
temperature can be provided automatically at all times.

Not only must the system of heating be determined as
soon as the shape of the building has been settled, but also
the exact position of the heating fittings must be considered
in relation to the known, or possible, situation of the
furniture. Intense heat will ruin books. Consequently there
should be a gap between the heating elements and any
shelves above them; there must also be asbestos beneath
such shelving.

Public rooms should be adequately ventilated even in the
coldest weather – few things are more unpleasant than having
to be for a long time in a heated building used by large
numbers of people where the air is stale. Efficient air control
(which is not provided in many modern buildings) and
properly designed and good air-conditioning avoid many
problems in this connexion. Two and more generations ago
it was customary to provide a fresh air grille with an easily
adjustable cover behind the radiators fixed to the walls.
This was a very effective method of adequately ventilating a
heated room without opening windows and so creating
draughts, but this method seems to have fallen into disuse.

The size of the department
The lending library should be big enough to seat as many
children as normally comprise a school class, plus 25 per cent,
at tables for not more than four each. To calculate the area

required, 25 square feet should be provided per child, plus a gangway of not less than 5 feet between the front of the wall shelving and the nearest tables or chairs.

Using these criteria, and assuming the average size of a class is 50, the total area is calculated as follows: fifty children plus 25% gives 62 children to be provided for at 25 sq.ft. per child, i.e. 1550 sq.ft. A room 39 feet square gives 1521 sq. feet, but as it is desirable to have 5 feet between wall shelving and tables the room should be 44 feet sq. This gives an area of 1936 sq.ft. and a wall run of 176 feet (44×4). To find the book capacity of this room, multiply 163 feet ($176 - 13$ for doorways) $\times$ 4 (shelves above one another) $\times$ 13 (books per foot) $= 8476$ books. This is a generous allocation, so some of the space can be used for book displays (of which there should be several) and a periodical display. It will also provide space for the shelving flat of picture books for small children.

The room should be large enough to accommodate all the books on open shelves around the walls. No alcoves should be provided, for these obstruct supervision, give the room the impression of being crowded and make it difficult to use the room satisfactorily for other purposes, after it is closed for the children's use, as sometimes has to be done.

The books for small boys and girls should be arranged separately from those for the older children. This can be done by placing them near the staff enclosure and arranging low book-cases not higher than three feet so as to form a separate area for the exclusive use of the smallest children. The reason for separating them in this way is that in some districts older boys and girls tend to tease smaller children. In the same way, part of the room can be reserved for consulting reference books, but for this purpose it is better to have a separate room fairly near the staff enclosure so as to provide supervision of the use of the materials. The children can then use the books without the interruption and distraction caused by others constantly passing by when choosing lending library books, or moving from one part of the room to another.

If the children's library is so large that the reference area (where books may be damaged or mutilated if not properly supervised) cannot be placed close to the staff enclosure, then it should be adjacent to the lending library but separated from it by a glazed screen or by book-cases, and oversight maintained by an assistant sitting at a desk or nearby in the lending library itself and acting as a readers' adviser. In a fairly large library where activities are carried on with the object of encouraging children to use books quite apart from their taking them home to read, and to engage in other activities, it is useful to have a separate activities room approximately twenty feet square. This can be furnished with collapsible tables and chairs so that it can be readily adapted for story hours and reading circles, dramatic, discussion or puppet making groups, etc. Cupboards, in which to keep tools, equipment and materials, should be in this room. It should have its entrance in the junior library but should also have an exit direct to the street, which could be used by both adults and children for activities taking place outside normal library hours.

The shape of the room

Although the shape of the room does not greatly matter, an oblong room is somewhat more convenient than one of any other shape. The staff enclosure should be at the middle of the long side of the room, just outside the room if it is in a large and busy library, or just inside if a medium-sized room. In a small library it is perhaps not necessary to have a specially built staff enclosure with exit and entrance sides: a table on which the trays of charges are kept and at which books are stamped, can be placed at the entrance to the room or the children's book-area. One member of staff can then observe all the children going in and out of the library and attend to them at this one table. If a separate children's room in a larger library is desirable then it is almost certain that a properly constructed staff enclosure will be needed.

In a large children's library it is possible to have a fairly large staff enclosure so that most of the clerical and routine work can be performed by the staff at work in that department. It is an advantage to have a small workroom nearby in which new books requiring processing (if a centralized cataloguing and processing department is not provided), or older books requiring re-binding, can be placed. Such a workroom should be close to the staff enclosure so that at busy times when additional staff are required for relief, assistants from it can appear immediately on being called by bell, buzzer or telephone. Staff should not be relegated to separate rooms to work in 'watertight' departments; it is especially desirable that senior members of the staff should not work in out-of-the-way places, because they are usually the most experienced, and if their duties include (as they ought) supervising the department they should always be available to readers when they are on duty. A much better place for the senior children's librarian is at a readers' adviser's desk in the centre of the library where she can supervise the children in the department, seeing that they put books away on the shelves tidily and use them properly. She is then available to give help and guidance in the choice of reading matter. In a busy library she should not be restricted to attending to children entering and leaving the library and to other duties in the staff enclosure. Her experience and knowledge should be at the disposal of the children in the library at all times; during slack periods, when there is book selection, preparation and other routine work to be dealt with, she can work at a table or a counter within the staff enclosure or in the workroom. But her main responsibility when the library is open is to see to the proper use of the library and the supervision of her assistants. When it is not absolutely necessary for her to work outside the junior library, she should be within it. These principles of library administration and supervision affect the planning of the library and the design of the furniture.

In a number of libraries cloak-rooms and toilet facilities are provided. Rooms for hanging outdoor clothes are desirable in cold or temperate climates where people enter a warm building from cold or wet conditions outside. Wet outdoor clothes are an encumbrance in the library, and if it is heated to 65° or 70°F, readers will wish to remove their outdoor garments. The increasing practice in modern libraries of providing cloakroom facilities raises problems of security. Although most libraries will not hold themselves responsible for personal belongings left in their charge, it is advisable to have an attendant available to receive coats, umbrellas, bags, baskets, etc., and to hand over a numbered ticket or other form of receipt for them, and to return them when the reader leaves the library, in exchange for the ticket. The problem also arises concerning the position in the building of the cloak-room and whether there should be separate ones for children and adults. In a large library it would be an advantage to have a cloak-room within the children's library so that as the children return their books they can pass into the cloak-room and hang up their coats; they would then choose their books, collect their coats and go out. This would reduce the possibility of unauthorised persons entering a cloak-room where there was no attendant. In a larger library one cloak-room, providing it was always staffed with an attendant, could serve both adults and children.

In some small libraries, coat hooks, shelves or even lockers for the use of readers are placed in entrance halls or other convenient places.

As it is considered essential to train children in the proper handling of books, the librarian must see that their hands are clean. It is quite a common practice for children to have to show their hands on entering a library; children whose hands are not clean enough to handle books can be shown into a small cloak-room where washing facilities are available. It is also an advantage to have lavatories for their exclusive use; separate accommodation should be provided for boys and girls where adults cannot have access.

Figure 9 is a plan of a suite of rooms for children in a large library: the lending library is reached from within the main entrance to the building. Children pass a cloakroom in which an attendant receives, over a counter, the possessions the children do not wish to take into the library. The staff enclosure is glazed on the passage side and unglazed on the opposite side at which the books are issued. Control of the children leaving is secured by a turnstile, part of which is under the counter. The wicket here, and one of those at the entrance, is operated by members of the staff not needing to use the controlled wickets. Very few libraries in western countries now in fact provide wickets or any form of control at the book-issuing and returning stage. The provision of such control is a matter of choice according to local conditions; in a very busy and/or understaffed library it would help to maintain order and reduce the theft of books. The staff enclosure is large enough to provide space for all the work needing to be done in the department as well as that concerned directly with the children. The provision of lavatories within the department ensures a measure of supervision by the children's librarian and prevents adults using same; it also avoids the necessity of sending children whose hands are not clean enough to handle books home to wash. The lending library is a desirable shape and can be completely supervised from the suitably placed staff enclosure, as can also the reference library which is separated from the lending library by a glazed screen above double-sided bookshelves. A low single-sided bookcase serves to form an exit passage. The activities room opens off the lending library and has a second door so that it can be entered or left by another street entrance or another part of the building when desired. This enables it to be used without opening up the children's library; it can also be divorced from this department when necessary and so provide accommodation for adult activities.

Decoration

The children's library should be gay but not bizarre. The style of decoration should not be obtrusive or 'juvenile'. Many older children resent using a library which is obviously decorated to cater for the taste of quite small children. Neither should the room be decorated in a contemporary fashion, for in a few years' time it may be 'out-dated'. Mural paintings should be avoided: as it is now customary to fasten plastic sleeves over the jackets of books there is no need to achieve colour through mural decoration – the books themselves provide enough.

The whole tenor of the children's library should be one in which the children may feel at ease. Variety of interest and colour can be provided by means of curtains, models of aeroplanes and ships, toys, pottery, glass, and vases of flowers. Such decoration should not be excessive, and if the top shelves of the book-cases have been filled in with cork-faced fronts for displaying cut-outs and notices, the library will be gay and attractive without objects on the tops of the book-cases. If there are fairly large wall spaces, however, framed pictures by well-known artists should be provided. They must not be so small as to look out of place, neither must they be so high as to be out of the children's line of vision.

Children's interest in natural history can be encouraged or extended by keeping fish in a glass tank or by having displays of flowers in season.

Floor coverings

The floor covering should be chosen to harmonize with the over-all decoration of the room.

As to the type of flooring material which may be used, there are many varieties but these are not all really suitable. Apart from marble (whether in the form of slabs, mosaic or terrazzo) the most hard-wearing are polyvinyl or thermo-plastic tiles. Other varieties of covering in use are carpet, linoleum, rubber and cork. The type of flooring used depends to some extent on the position of the children's library in the building, and the climatic conditions of the country. Consideration must be given to the amount of dirt which is likely to enter the library. In temperate countries and in those where monsoons occur, where there is much dust, dirt or rain, it is inevitable that dirt will tread into the library and the problem of keeping it clean is a very important one.

'Terrazzo' or 'mosaic' is the best form of flooring to have immediately inside the entrance hall because this can be cleaned with water containing detergent and scrubbed if necessary without harming the floor. It has the further advantage of not needing polishing. There is one practical point to bear in mind when there is a mosaic or terrazzo floor, and that is that when it is next to a polished floor people wearing shoes without rubber heels are almost sure to slip ; there is then the possibility of claims for injury. Any floor reached directly from the street should be covered with link mats made of coconut fibre or rubber – and even then some dirt will tread into the room.

The type of floor covering used should be one which, if it has to be washed, will not come away from the basic floor. Marble, cement, terrazzo, mosaic and wood are all basic floors which may be left without a covering, but marble, terrazzo and mosaic are the only ones which *never* have a covering put on them. Washing is almost sure to cause rubber, thermoplastic, polyvinyl, or linoleum to come unstuck eventually. These last four materials should only be used in positions where they will not need to be cleaned with water. Similarly, cork should never be used except in rooms a long way from the street entrance because this disintegrates very quickly if it becomes wet.

One of the chief reasons for using linoleum, in addition to its good lasting qualities, is that it is quiet. Quietness is as essential in a children's library as it is in an adult reference library. Children are naturally noisy, and quite apart from the sound made by their voices, they often run noisily. It is therefore essential that the quietest form of floor covering should be used. In this respect linoleum and particularly carpet are best. Some of the most durable floor covering materials are the noisiest.

Cork, linoleum, thermoplastic and polyvinyl floors are kept in best condition if they are lightly polished frequently. Should they become dirty, either with too much polish or with dirt trodden in, they should be cleaned with a turps substitute or a cleaner recommended by the manufacturer. The best of these materials are undoubtedly linoleum, thermoplastic or vinyl, the latter two having better wearing qualities.

In recent years, especially in America, carpeting has been used in school class-rooms and libraries, and reports state that it is as durable, and no more expensive than other floor coverings. It is certainly the quietest, and is easy to clean.

It is inadvisable because of cost of materials, to use a thin flooring material when a thicker is available. The additional cost of labour and the higher cost of material in years to come when renewal is required far outweigh the extra cost of slightly thicker materials in the first instance. It is also advisable to have a flooring laid in smallish squares rather than in long sheets, because there are certain parts of every room which receive more wear than others, and the floor covering at the parts where much wear occurs can be replaced by taking up the worn squares and sticking down new ones of the same colour and pattern in their place. Such repairs are very noticeable where the original floor covering was laid in sheets, but where it was laid in squares, renewals are seldom noticed.

Thermoplastic, polyvinyl, rubber, linoleum and cork may all be stuck to basic floors of other materials, such as wood or concrete. It is essential however to make sure if the basic floor is on the ground that dampness cannot rise, otherwise the adhesive will be ineffective and the covering come away. This can be achieved by applying a sealer to the floor before laying the floor covering.

It is also essential to see that the basic floor is absolutely level and clean. Screeding lines caused during the laying of a concrete floor, or grit left on it, or unevennesses in a wooden floor, will all show through to the surface of the covering; not only will the appearance be unsatisfactory but the covering will wear rapidly where ridged.

Whatever kind of material is used, it is advisable not to have plain colours, but to have a mottled pattern in several colours chosen to harmonize with those used in the room decoration. Plain colours show footmarks very easily, and if there is any slight difference in the shade of pieces used for repair these will be noticeable, whereas if there are slight variations in the colouring of mottled materials they are likely to be less conspicuous. Also, such a material will enable a change of colour scheme to be provided when the room is redecorated without it looking unsuitable with the floor covering.

So far, little reference has been made to wood, but it undoubtedly makes a most satisfactory floor. Hard woods, either local or imported, are available in all countries, and if these are properly seasoned, and fixed by hidden nailing through tongues, they are extremely durable. Here again they should only be used where it is not necessary to clean by washing; they are kept in the best condition by lightly polishing. Wood has a disadvantage of being noisy in countries where people use leather shoes without rubber heels, or wooden shoes, or shoes studded with metal, because of the annoyance which can be caused by the noise of people walking about on it.

THE FURNITURE

Once the building or room has been constructed, the comfort of those using it depends very largely on the design of the furniture placed in it. The architect needs to know the kind of furniture that is to go into the spaces he plans, for both building and furniture complement each other. If the architect is capable of designing good furniture (and not all architects – even famous ones – are able to do this) it might make for a more homogeneous building. Furniture need not be custom-made but it must not be unsuitable for the style of architecture used. Standard furniture can be satisfactory and cheaper than custom-made, especially if the manufacturer of the latter is not a specialist in furniture-making. The important thing is to make sure that the furniture for a children's library is of a suitable size and simple in design.

SHELVING

Shelving should be placed around the walls only: island shelving should not be used except for purposes of display as it tends to obstruct supervision of the room; alcoves are equally unsatisfactory for the same reason. Moreover, unless free-standing and not longer than six feet, shelves restrict the rearrangement of furniture. When the room is planned, the usable wall space should be enough to accommodate on open shelves all the books that will be needed.

For the smallest children

Every children's library has to cater for children from four to fourteen years of age. It is therefore necessary to provide not only a variety of books but also shelving of different dimensions. Shelves must accommodate fairly large numbers of quite small and thin books for the smallest children, and also large (and sometimes thin) books for these and for the older ones. It will also be necessary to provide about a twelfth of the total shelving capacity for books over 10 inches high, the minimum height of a quarto book. Octavo books are up to 10 inches high, and quartos are between 10 inches and 13 inches high and folios 13 inches and over. Accommodation for very few folios will be needed, however; not more than half-a-dozen atlases, perhaps. Because a high proportion of the books for the smallest children are so thin that it is impossible to put the titles on the spines, the current tendency is to keep them flat on sloping shelves. This is usually done by using a bracket type of shelving – that is, with each shelf resting on a bracket – but at an angle of from 15° to about 75° to the vertical, each shelf being placed above another and each being more upright than the one below. Not more than three shelves are possible for the small children, or some will be out of reach. Such bookcases (but with more shelves) can be used for thin books for the older children. All sloping shelves must have a ledge projecting half an inch to prevent books falling off. This is an extravagant way of displaying books in terms of shelf footage but it will be appreciated that a library with its books arranged in this way is not only a very much more colourful and attractive room, but children are able to see the titles of the books very much more easily and they will be attracted to them much more readily. The same method of display is an advantage in countries where locally produced books are usually paper-bound and without titles on the spine. As a matter of convenience it is advisable to have the small,

thin books for the youngest members of the library separate
from the others. Adjustable shelving will enable far more of
this kind to be kept in a tier than if mixed up with larger ones.
It is essential, however, with all thin books which are kept on
the shelves in the ordinary way, that the shelves should not
be longer from left to right than 12 inches, otherwise the
books will tend to slide down, and in addition to looking
untidy, will be difficult to manage on the shelves.

Design for adaptability

It is possible for the character of a district to change considerably over the years so that shelving which was suitable
in the children's library at the time it was built, may be
needed for books for adults in fifteen or twenty years' time.
Therefore the shelves should be designed in such a way that
they can be easily adapted as necessary. It looks well if the
top of the book-cases are the same height all the way round
the room. The bottom shelf should not be lower than 11
inches from the floor, and the spacing between shelves
worked out at 10 inches clear when designing the shelving. If
there are four shelves of this kind with a 3 inch cornice the
total height of the fitting will be 4 feet 9 inches, providing
the bottom shelf is 11 inches from the floor. This will also
allow five shelves at 8 inches to be provided – enough for the
usual run of story books. These dimensions allow for 1 inch
thick shelves. The top of these bookcases may seem low, but the
chief aim is to provide a library which will be comfortable
for most of the readers. The ages at which children in a
literate society make most use of the library are 8 to 11 or 12,
and if we cater for these when designing the shelving, and
fill in the top shelf where the books for children under 8 are
to be shelved, or provide specially low cases for them, no
one will be inconvenienced. English children of 8 to 11 years
of age are between 4 feet 5 inches and 4 feet 9 inches in height:
the titles on the top shelf of a book-case, the top of which is

4 feet 9 inches from the floor, are therefore roughly level with their eyes. Where it is intended to arrange books for the smallest children in book-cases of this height, the top shelf in this run can be filled in with a cork covered framework which can serve as a display panel for tier guides, cutouts, coloured pictures, etc. This can be hinged at the top and the top shelf can then serve as a cupboard for reserve books, illustrations, books needing binding, lettering materials, etc. In order to make the shelves even more adaptable, instead of hingeing this framework, if two dowels are fixed at the bottom and two at the top of the framework, these can negotiate holes in the underneath edge of the cornice and also in the top shelf. The display panels can then be taken out and put back at will. It is then easily possible to extend or reduce, according to varying demand, the amount of shelving available for readers of different age groups.

It may be considered that if shelves are no higher than 4 feet 9 inches (the bottom of the top shelf being about 3 feet 10 inches from the floor) this is too low and a considerable amount of space thereby wasted. It is true that a fourth more books could be put in the room if there were an extra shelf all the way round, but the top shelf at this height is reasonably convenient for most of the children who are likely to use the library; an extra shelf would be too high for most of the 8 to 11 year olds who form the bulk of the members. The top of the book-case, if it is not higher than 5 feet, can be used for displaying book jackets, books, models, pottery or glass effectively and satisfactorily, and the whole impression of the room will be more satisfying than if the shelves are higher and such displays not possible.

Another idea is to have the top shelf approximately 3 feet 6 inches from the floor and instead of having it horizontal, to have it sloping at an angle of about 55°–60° with a ledge in front so that books can be displayed flat on it. Such sloping tops should be at least 9 inches deep. A bookcase of this kind should not be placed adjoining higher shelving or it will look unsightly.

The length of shelf from left to right should not be greater than 36 inches and all the shelving throughout the library, except for thin books for younger readers and for quartos, should be of the standard length in order to enable shelves to be used in any part of the building where there is the same depth of shelf, and so enable the rearrangement of books to be carried out conveniently as and when desirable. The exception to this length of shelf is where thin books or quartos are used, in which case all the shelves should be 12 inches from left to right.

If a run of the 3 foot shelves will not fit exactly into the length of wall, the remaining shelves should be as long as the space available; this is better than dividing the whole length equally, as this would make the interchangeability of shelves impossible. Shelves should not be shorter by $\frac{1}{2}$ inch than the distance between uprights, otherwise they may ride out easily, or be so short as to fall between the supports.

Steel v. wood

The choice of steel or wood for shelving and other furniture is largely a matter of personal taste.

Steel has certain advantages and disadvantages. The advantages are: (a) it does not warp or twist with humidity or age unless it is loaded in excess of the weight it was designed to carry; (b) it is impervious to insects and termites; nevertheless, shelves should be dusted with an anti-insect powder such as DDT, or painted with an anti-insect fluid to prevent breeding and damage to books due to insects being in the dust on the shelves or in the books when shelved; (c) its high tensile strength enables slightly thinner uprights to be used than in the case of wood; the difference is so slight however that the larger number of books which steel shelves can accommodate, compared with wood, is negligible.

The disadvantages are: (a) the 'paint' on the most carefully prepared and finished steel will chip if knocked, or wear away in tropical climates where it comes into contact with moist hands, even in air-conditioned rooms; (b) it does not give so 'warm' and pleasant an impression as wood, even when painted in colours other than olive green; (c) it is probably much more expensive than wood if it has to be imported after fabrication; (d) it is especially expensive if dimensions depart from standard sizes; such departure is desirable sometimes to save space, e.g. standard shelf depth is 8 inches whereas it need only be 6 inches for octavo books. To achieve individuality, and make special provision such as cork display panels at the top of the cases, is almost impossible.

Wood has the following advantages: (a) it has a pleasing texture and gives an impression of 'warmth' and richness that is impossible with steel; (b) fabrication is possible in any country, using local timbers; (c) it can be 'purpose-made', and the utmost advantage taken of available space.

Disadvantages are: (a) insects can eat into it in tropical countries unless it is tanalized; (b) it will warp unless it is carefully chosen for quality, properly seasoned, and of the right dimensions.

When going out to tender for steel furniture, it is necessary to specify exactly the thickness of the steel to be used and also the processes to be used in preparing the material to prevent rust, and for the final finishing. Details of the processes will be supplied by reputable manufacturers. When buying standard furniture the purchaser needs to know this information in order to be able to assess the merits of each make offered. Shelving uprights should be at least 16 gauge (·0598″ or 1·5 mm.) and shelves 18 gauge (·0478″ or 1·2 mm.) if not longer than three feet. If the steel is not thick enough, the shelves will bend with the weight of books. Reliable manufacturers who specialize in library shelving can be counted on to ensure that there are no sharp or rough edges anywhere on which fingers or books may be damaged. Detailed specifications have to be drawn up if non-specialists are likely to tender, and examples of their work will have to be examined carefully before acceptance of a tender. It would be advisable also to see that the shelving is examined during the course of manufacture to ensure that the specification is being complied with. The steel of some library shelving on the market is thinner than these recommendations.

Standard steel shelving should never be used unless it is book shelving specially made to give immediate adjustability. Shelving of the storage type which requires the loosening of screws or of nuts should under no circumstances be used for books; for not only is the time taken in altering the position of the shelves considerable, but also the nuts can damage the books, and the uprights usually have a flange behind which the end books on a shelf can be hidden.

If wood is used, a hardwood should be chosen and it must be properly seasoned or dried (either by air or kiln) and tanalized (subjected to impregnation by chemicals under great pressure) or otherwise treated to prevent damage by white ants and other insects if it is likely to be used where there is a possibility of such infestation. If it is not possible to use all hardwood, soft wood may be used but with the front inch of hardwood. Shelving should never be less than $\frac{7}{8}$ inch thick, and an inch thick is preferable.

Under no circumstances should grilles or glass doors be fixed to book-cases in open-access libraries except to prevent unauthorised handling when the library is used for other purposes, for books should be readily available on the open access system to all comers. Even in countries where the standard of honesty with regard to other people's property is low, and consequently people consider that they can appropriate public library books, the shelves should be open and the users of the library encouraged and taught to respect the ownership of library books. In places where considerable mutilation of books occurs, either by writing in them, tearing out pages or even the whole of the book leaving only the cover on the shelf, these practices should be discouraged by adequate supervision, and by reprimanding or punishing offenders either by charging fines for the replacement of the books or by preventing the persons responsible from using the library.

Adjustability

Shelves should be adjustable. This is required chiefly in order to make it possible to rearrange the spacing of shelves at will and so vary the accommodation available for small books or large books as required. If fixed shelves are provided (at least one well-known librarian has in recent years reverted to the out-moded principle of fixed shelving, on the grounds that such shelving is cheaper, and that it is in fact seldom necessary to alter the position of shelves in order to accommodate books of different sizes), it will never be possible to rearrange the position of books of various kinds or sizes without waste of space between shelves. This makes it difficult in the future when changing usage of the library, or a variation in the amount of shelving needed for octavos or quartos or duodecimos, make rearrangement necessary. Adjustability is much more necessary in a children's library than in an adult lending library or reference library because of the greater variety in the heights of books and also in the fluctuation over the years in the need for books of different kinds because of the variation in the number of children of different ages using the library, and to meet changes in publishing fashions.

The insertion of wooden or metal pins in holes bored in the uprights, or of wooden strips placed in grooves cut into uprights are not satisfactory means of providing adjustability of shelves, largely because the wooden or metal pins may not be easy to replace once lost, or the degree of adjustability is not great enough. Pieces of wood which rest in notches cut in uprights fastened towards the front and back of the sides of uprights are also unsatisfactory because the degree of adjustability they provide is insufficient. At least 1 inch adjustability should be provided: some standard fittings allow $\frac{3}{4}$ inch or $\frac{5}{8}$ inch adjustability. Two well-known and satisfactory makes of adjustable shelf fittings are Lundia (a Swedish method which is used in shelving made under licence in many parts of the world), and Tonks of Birmingham.

The Lundia system consists of holes bored at 1 inch (or less) intervals and about 1 inch from the front and from the back of the uprights. Into the holes are placed the ends of a U-shaped horizontal metal rod, the ends turning away from the rod only just enough for it to be secure in the holes. The slotted ends of the shelves, are pushed on to the rods after they have been placed in position in the uprights. When the shelves are in position nothing of the rods can be seen. Shelves fixed in this way will not move until drawn out intentionally, and they can support several hundredweight. It is essential that the wood should be thoroughly seasoned and not likely to shrink, also that the work of drilling the holes should be done with great precision, otherwise the metal rods will not be level. Such fittings are not suitable when cupboard doors exist as they prevent the shelves being slid horizontally over the metal rods (except when specially fitted to allow for this). This circumstance arises with most forms of fitting.

The Tonks fittings consist of metal strips about $\frac{3}{4}$ inch wide with slots cut in them at $\frac{3}{4}$ inch or 1 inch intervals. The shelf uprights are rabbeted to take the metal strips so that when fixed they are flush with the uprights. One design of strips is such that they can be screwed to the upright from which they project. This is not really suitable for book-cases as books would push against the strips; little, if any, damage can be caused, however, because the strips are well made and have no sharp edges. Small studs on which the shelves rest are placed in the slots in the uprights. It is important to see that the strips are fixed carefully so that the slots are opposite one another, otherwise the shelves will not be perfectly level when in position. These little studs have points where they come into contact with the underside of the shelves thus helping to secure them. The strips must not be placed further than 1 inch from the front edge of the upright or the shelves may tip forward.

Other aspects of shelving design

Twenty-five years ago the practice of sloping the lowest or the lower two shelves of a tier developed in order to make it easier for people to read the titles on these shelves and so avoid both eye-strain and stooping. This causes difficulties in design, sometimes resulting in ugly ended island stacks, and takes up about 4 inches of gangway space in front of each bookcase (8 inches in the case of each island stack). Since those days it has become common practice to raise the bottom shelf to a distance of anything from 12 inches to 18 inches from the floor thus lessening the difficulty of seeing the titles of books there. Also, better lighting due to fluorescent fittings, has so much improved the general standard of lighting in libraries that it is now easier to see the titles. In a children's library, there is no need to slope the shelves because the lowest shelf is relatively near the children's eye level.

Although sloping shelves are useful in adult libraries, they are not necessary in children's libraries. There are a number of United Kingdom children's libraries which were built soon after the last war which have them, however. One reason for this is that for some extraordinary reason shelves which were sloped were devoid of purchase tax –

although they used more wood and were more intricate to make and therefore took longer and cost more! In a one-room library, it would not look pleasing to have sloping book-cases for the adults and straight ones for the children.

It is desirable that the space between the bottom shelf and the floor should be filled in rather than left open because an open space not only allows dirt and dust to collect, but polishers and brooms will inevitably damage the edges of the uprights supporting the shelves. If this space is filled in the library will look neater and be cleaner.

Local construction

There are a number of points to be borne in mind if wooden shelving has to be constructed locally because the reputable specialists in library furniture are so far away that shipping and other transport charges make the best quality furniture too expensive. Local cabinet-makers sometimes do not realize the importance of extreme accuracy in measurements and workmanship which are achieved automatically in an efficient machine shop. Sometimes one of the results is that all shelves are not inter-changeable. They must be exact to $\frac{1}{32}$ inch and *all* uprights must be fixed at *exact* distances apart, otherwise shelves cannot be inter-changed at will. Extreme accuracy must also be exercised in securing the fittings used to achieve adjustability, otherwise the shelves will not be level. The following points should be insisted upon in ad-dition to the wood being properly seasoned and dried to prevent warping: (a) it must be free from sap, knots, splits, holes (including pin and bore holes made by insects), and other defects; (b) no shelves should be longer than 36 inches; (c) when 'finished', uprights and shelves should be $\frac{7}{8}$ inch thick or 1 inch if hardwood is not used; this is to prevent sagging and twisting; (d) the exposed surfaces should be wax-polished, lacquered or french-polished as an additional preservative and to give a good finish; (e) adjustable fittings,

or supports for unfixed shelves, should be not more than
1 inch from the front and back of the uprights, otherwise
the shelves may tip and upset the books.

No backing is needed if shelving is to be placed against
a wall – the circulation of air is beneficial for the books —
or for back-to-back shelving.

Wooden shelves should not be painted (book jackets
give sufficient colour to a room) as this will inevitably mean
that all books will have to be taken off the shelves to avoid
damage during painting, and the library will have to be
closed while the work is being done.

Shelf capacity

If it is required to calculate the total length of shelving
required for a given number of books, divide the stock by
13 (10 for reference books) which is the number of books
that can be accommodated in a foot run of shelving. If it is
anticipated that the total stock needing to be provided on
open shelves will be higher in years to come, appropriate
allowance should be made at this early stage, otherwise a
room for 'reserve' books will be needed. If this is not done,
the shelves will one day either be over full or books will have
to be disposed of sooner than necessary. When shelves are
more than five-sixths full, arranging the books in order and
inserting others begins to get difficult.

Shelving in relation to windows

When planning the library it is an advantage to utilize
almost the whole of the wall space for books and to keep the
window-sills at least one foot above the top of the book-cases,
especially in latitudes where the angle of the sun can be very
low and where bright sunlight will penetrate and make it
difficult to see the titles of books on the shelves because of the
strong light shining in the eyes. For aesthetic reasons, an
occasional low window is an advantage if the views from it

are attractive. Books and furniture should not be placed beneath it, however, except perhaps a bench seat or one shelf of books so sloped that the spines are at an angle of about 30°, and about 2 feet or less from the floor.

The furniture which stands about the room should be limited to tables, chairs, periodical cases and an occasional display fitting. This will then make it possible to use the room sometimes for other purposes such as story hours, discussion groups, play readings, talks, etc. if no lecture hall is available. In certain circumstances it may be desirable to use it for public functions for those who are not necessarily members of the children's library; in this case none of the junior library staff would be on duty in the room to protect the books against damage and unauthorized borrowing. It would therefore be necessary to have spring-roller blinds or grilles of some kind in front of the book-cases so that the books could not be handled. Experience has shown that where the stock consists largely of books in limp covers, especially if they are thin ones, or are even thin books bound in boards, it is desirable that the metal grille should be of very small mesh metal, and also to see that it cannot be prised away, even temporarily, from the book-cases.

OTHER FURNITURE

Tables

It is an advantage to have both round and oblong tables in a room for the sake of variety in appearance. They should be of two or three heights to accommodate children of different sizes. The area of the table-top should not be too big, neither should the tables be so heavy that two average-sized children cannot easily move them. The British Standards Institution has undertaken researches into the height, shape and sizes of tables and chairs to suit the different heights of children, and the following recommendations are given as a result of their researches:

Height of child	Code	Height of tables	Height of chair seats
44″ – 47″	A	19½″	11″
48″ – 52″	B	21½″	12½″
54″ – 56″	C	23½″	14″
58″ – 62″	D	25½″	15½″
64″	E	27½″	17½″

These recommendations, together with recommended designs, are given in BS. 3030 Part 3, 1959: *School furniture Part 3: Pupil's classroom chairs and tables*, and are based on B.S. anthropometric recommendation. An analysis of the children attending schools in Britain resulted in the following:

Kind of school	Average height of pupils		Percentage of tables needed according to height
Infants, mixed	46″	A	75%
Age 5–7 incl.	(44″ – 48″)	B	25%
Junior, mixed	52″	B	55%
Age 7–11 incl.	(50″ – 56″)	C	45%
Secondary, mixed	60″	C	30%
Age 11–15 incl.	(56″ – 64″)	D	70%
Secondary, boys	60″	D	75%
Age 11–15 incl.	(56″ – 64″)	E	25%
Secondary, girls	60″	C	30%
Age 11–15 incl.	(56″ – 62″)	D	70%

This should be a fairly reliable guide to the proportion of tables of different heights for use in a library in any country, but the above-mentioned measurements should be consulted in relation to statistics of heights of local children when deciding on the provision of tables and chairs. When the heights of children (75% Chinese) in Singapore were compared with the full tables as given in the B.S. it was found that girls under 10 were sometimes taller than boys, whereas in England they are the same height until 14, after which age both the English and the Chinese children follow the same age-height development pattern, boys growing more rapidly than girls. The Chinese children are 3 inches to 4 inches smaller than the English children throughout the ages of 6 to 18. An analysis of members of the library which was undertaken by means of punched cards based on information given on application cards showed that there were far more members among boys than girls at all ages. Enquiries of this nature are extremely useful in determining the appropriate numbers of tables and chairs of different sizes that should be provided.

The number of tables of each size needed will depend not only on factors of this kind, but also on the number of children of each age *using* the library or expected to use it, as distinct from members enrolled throughout the system as a whole. For example, in a district where there are schools attended by children of secondary school age and few primary schools, whether the district is a residential one or not, there should be a higher proportion of the largest size of table than in a library where there is no secondary school in the vicinity. The tops of tables should not be larger than 30 inches by 52 inches, and round tables should be 40 inches or 42 inches in diameter.

The surface of the table is also important; it has been found that where reading is done continuously, light colours and shiny surfaces are a disadvantage – light colours because of the reflection of light causing a certain amount of eye strain, and the shiny surface because it increases reflection. Plastic materials of the Formica type are excellent for tables as well as counter tops because of their durability, and these can now be obtained with a matt surface; linoleum is a suitable material for table tops because of its non-reflection quality, but its surface can be damaged more easily, though not by normal wear. Solid wooden tops are the cheapest, but warping or cracking through shrinkage is almost sure to occur unless blockboard is used. Even when plastic or linoleum surfaces are used these should be bonded under great pressure to wood laminate, or an especially good adhesive used.

The corners of the tables and the outer edges of the legs should be rounded so that the reader's legs cannot be hurt – one contemporary style has completely round or oval legs. There should be no cross rails or rails between the legs except very near the top of the table as they get in the way of readers' feet, become scratched, and tempt children to stand on them. It is best if legs are secured to table tops so as to avoid both rails and aprons, for these get in the way of readers' knees. Tables without rails or aprons need a centre stretcher, and very strong leg-top joint or metal fixing to ensure that there is no possibility that the legs will become loose, otherwise the table will vibrate when used for writing or typing. Before tables without rails or aprons are purchased it is advisable to carry out a thorough investigation to make sure that they are constructed soundly and that they have been proved to be sturdy.

Chairs

Chairs should be of simple design with no rails between the legs lower than 3 inches below the seat, and of a height which matches the height of the tables as indicated on p. 187. The British Standards Institution recommends putting a small colour symbol, a different colour for each related size, on both chairs and tables to make sure that those of the appropriate sizes are placed together.

In temperate climates, chairs with upholstered seat and

back look well and are comfortable. But in tropical and humid climates (except for use in air-conditioned rooms), solid material, either wood or steel (but preferably wood because metal inevitably rusts in time) is preferable. In rooms which are not air-conditioned, cane seats and backs are most suitable because of the greater degree of ventilation which they allow. The cane is not very durable, however, and has to be renewed, though this is not an expensive process.

One of the advantages of upholstery is that it does away with the institutional feeling that wooden, metal or some plastic furniture tends to give. We want children to have a feeling of homeliness in the library so that they look upon it as a place which they are welcome to use with supervised freedom, and in which they may browse. There is now a great variety of upholstery materials, and the qualities which should be looked for are (a) resistance to wear, (b) resistance to staining, (c) ease of cleaning, and (d) fastness of colour to light and dampness. Leather and some natural fabrics do not stand up so well to some of these requirements – particularly the last – as some of the synthetic materials. Some of these materials have the softness and texture of natural fabrics; they are either coated plastics with a fabric texture impressed in the surface, or they are woven from plastic or extremely durable synthetic fibres. In the latter case they have the desirable 'breathing' qualities of natural fibres. The filling used for upholstered seats and backs should be best quality kapok, cotton, curled hair or foam rubber. The last is best as it keeps its shape, is resilient indefinitely, and (what is very important in some districts and in tropical countries) does not harbour insects or vermin. The rubber should however be 100% pure latex, as inferior grades may contain clay which invariably crumbles in time and causes loss of resilience.

The shape, size and angle of the seat, the shape of the

back of the chair, and the position and angle of the bottom back back rail, if one is provided, are important. Details in this connexion may be found in the British Standard No. 3030, Part 3.

The design of the chairs, and indeed of all the furniture, should be simple and devoid of all mouldings, ledges, carvings and other kinds of ornamentation which require excessive cleaning or repairing. Arms of chairs should be low enough to go under the tables (this is another reason for the tables having no apron), and if they are likely to be placed against the walls, as in a lecture hall or activities room, the rear legs should project beyond the back of the chair so that the back does not damage the walls.

No 'domes of silence' should be used on the chairs for the purpose of preventing damage to the floorcovering which a square sharp-edged bottom of the chair-leg may cause, as these (although an advantage from the point of view of quietness) cause indentations in most floors. A better means of achieving quietness and avoiding damage to the floor covering is to use a rubber cushion secured to the bottom of the chair-legs. It is essential, however, to have the chairs examined from time to time to see that worn cushions are replaced, otherwise the screws which secure them, or the ends of metal legs from which cushions have come off, may damage the floor. If such protectors are used care should be taken to see that the height of the chair-seat in relation to table height is not increased.

Easy chairs of the armchair type provide a less formal atmosphere in the library. These can be arranged singly or in groups and look quite well if placed around low 'coffee' tables. They are particularly favoured by small children, and even by older children who have really grown beyond the stage of needing small chairs. They can be painted to add attractiveness to the library, but they will need re-painting from time to time.

The use of painted shelves or furniture generally in children's libraries is not recommended because the paint wears off in a short time, and re-painting is expensive.

Settees, or benches can be provided with advantage at windows or walls, or around pillars supporting the ceiling. These may be upholstered, or cane-seated according to climatic conditions, and should match the rest of the furniture.

In recent years the use of benches and stools without backs has become a fashion in some countries. Many years ago it was decided that for comfort, children should not be made to sit on benches or stools but should be provided with seats with backs, unless their lodgment was only for a few minutes. Seats without backs are not comfortable and tend to cause those using them to sit with curved spines. If seating is to be provided it should be comfortable. All benches and settees should therefore have backs, even if only a wall or pillar. One reason for the use of benches is said to be that more children can be accommodated in a given space than on chairs. This is true, but even so, the greater accommodation should not be provided at the expense of the children's comfort, and also at the expense of the lack of discipline which is bound to occur when children are crowded together on benches.

Tables with sloping tops
Another useful piece of furniture is a table with a sloping top, or a narrow desk or bench with a sloping top so that large volumes such as atlases and big dictionaries can be consulted while standing up. Very large folio volumes are best shelved in atlas cabinets with pull-out shelves, one volume on each shelf.

Periodical racks
Periodicals should be provided in every children's library,

for their short articles, stories, jokes and snippets of news serve as a quite useful introduction to more sustained reading, as well as being topical and informative. It is an advantage to display them on specially made fittings rather than to leave them loose on tables where they are in the way of people needing to use the tables. They also tend to give an impression of untidiness if left on tables, especially if not in periodical cases.

There are five kinds of periodical display fitting, varying in design according to the necessity either to display periodicals attractively or to arrange them in as compact a space as possible. If the intention is to attract attention to the periodicals and to encourage their use, which is usual in any children's library, they should be displayed with as much of the cover showing as possible. The best way is to arrange a series of supports one behind the other, 12 inches high, 1½ inches apart and at an angle of about 70° from the horizontal, the bottom of each support being 4 inches below, and behind, the top of the one in front of it. There is a piece of wood 1½ inches deep between each support and on this the periodicals rest. These fittings can be made as long as desired, and as many supports can be placed behind one another as is convenient. The bottom one, however, should not be lower than 12 inches from the floor and the top one should be one foot below the top of the fitting which should be lower than the bookcases. These can be made as double display fittings, that is, with periodicals on both sides, or they can be made single, and placed back to back or against a wall. It is essential that the slope of the back against which the periodicals rest should be at an angle of about 70° to the horizontal in order that the periodicals do not flop forward and so obscure themselves or those displayed on the shelf below.

In order to make it possible to rearrange the furniture of the room when necessary, or provide additional display fittings without their looking as if they are not part of the original furnishings, moveable periodical cases are preferable to wall fittings. If units are 3 feet 6 inches long they will just take four of the widest periodicals side by side.

The display of periodicals without inserting them in protective cases adds colour and attractiveness to a room and is strongly recommended, although they become dog-eared a little sooner. These cases can be of strawboard covered entirely with plastic, leather-cloth or leather, or they can have a thick rigid, transparent plastic front. Both kinds suffer from inherent disadvantages, the corners of the first can be easily bent if the cases are dropped, and after a time those with plastic fronts, clear when they are new, become opaque. Cases are usually provided with a cord or tape to hold the periodical in position, but these tend to break the back of thick periodicals. The cost of substantial covers with a thick transparent front is high in relation to the cost of the periodicals. It will be found that the covers of periodicals do not come off very much more rapidly when they are not placed in cases. Running a paste brush down the inside cover of a periodical where it joins the first and last page of advertisements or text, and covering the spine or fold of the cover with adhesive transparent tape, will help to prevent the covers coming off or wearing away at the spine.

Card catalogue cabinets

No piece of library furniture needs greater precision in its manufacture than the card catalogue cabinet. The cards must lie at the right angle, must move easily over the rod provided to prevent them from being removed by readers, and must not be pinched by a too-narrow drawer. The catch which prevents the drawers from being removed from the cabinet accidentally, and yet allows them to be easily removed when necessary must be well designed and operated without difficulty. The drawers must glide smoothly and without restriction. Cabinets which have been made in recent years by some firms who can make ordinary furniture well are so unsatisfactory in use that the conclusion must be drawn that they are such difficult things to make that they should be bought only from firms which have specialised in them for many years.

Even if well-made catalogue cabinets are copied exactly there may be difficulty in obtaining the most suitable fittings. The design of drawer fronts has improved considerably in recent years, particularly in restricting the number of fittings; the rod is secured at the back of the drawer, and a "pull" is avoided by sloping the front and placing a groove at its lower edge.

Staff enclosure

A place must be provided in every children's library where books may be issued and received when they have been finished with, and where borrowers can be registered. This piece of furniture may be a simple table, a counter, a desk, or a large staff enclosure, according to the size of the children's library. As the staff is usually small in number and quite often there is only one assistant on duty at a time the staff enclosure should be in as central and accessible a place as possible. It should not be bigger than is absolutely necessary, for if there is only one person on duty that person wants to be able to discharge and issue books (which comprises most of her work at busy times) with the minimum amount of movement from one place to another. It is best to have children entering and leaving the library at different sides of the staff enclosure so as to avoid confusion. The counter should not be as tall as the adult one, in fact the counter top should not be higher than 2 feet 4 inches. This is much lower than counters are normally made, but is recommended as being more suitable from the children's point of view, and also to enable the assistants to sit down while dealing with the children – this has an advantage for the children as well as for the assistants. The entrance side of the staff enclosure should have a sloping shelf along its length at an angle of about 30° to the horizontal and sloping inwards, on which children may place the books they are returning. The shelf will need a ledge on the staff side to prevent books from slipping on to the issue trays placed on the counter top between it and the assistant. The public side of this shelf should be 9 inches, and the staff side $5\frac{1}{2}$ inches, above the counter top. It should be covered with a plastic material such as Formica, or linoleum, as it will receive considerable wear. The counter tops should also be covered with the same material, for they too will be subjected to continuous hard wear. The material should not be shiny, or light in colour, as this will reflect light and so cause fatigue to the assistants' eyes. The counter at the entrance side of the staff enclosure will need two drawers with locks, and a fines box should be provided at a suitable position so that the fines may be placed in it. The type of box normally provided has a glass or plastic top with a slot through which coins are dropped. They fall on to a small hinged horizontal base or shelf, and when it is agreed by both borrower and assistant that the amount is correct, a lever is pressed and the little shelf on which the coins rest is lowered at one side and the coins fall into the drawer or box underneath. A spring fixed underneath the shelf causes it to rise to a horizontal position as soon as pressure on the lever is released.

Shelves will be required underneath these counters to take returned books or books requiring repair or rebinding, or for books which have been reserved by readers. Cupboards will also be required to accommodate stores, stationery, record books, etc. The exit side of the counter is similar, except that the shelf on which returned books are placed, and the fines box, are not necessary. Drawers for membership cards and similar records are usefully kept at another side of the enclosure.

Book display

Children need to be attracted to books, and in order to achieve this, either the books themselves, or book jackets, are usually exhibited in conspicuous positions. If the design of the shelves includes a cork-faced front at the top shelf position, book jackets can be pinned to these, otherwise they can be put on a notice-board or a screen. They should be arranged attractively in a pattern, and not placed as close as possible in order to get the maximum number in the available display space.

The tops of book-cases (providing they are not so high as to be difficult to see), can be used for the display of books themselves, but the most usual method is to have a selection on a topic and stand them up on ordinary shelves placing a subject heading or caption on the top shelf. Such headings should be done in colour, free hand, by a poster artist; if a drawing or design can be incorporated, this will make them all the more attractive.

Books can also be displayed in troughs on the counter top or on tables.

In some libraries special fittings are provided for the display of books. These usually consist of the equivalent of troughs but are, of course, immoveable. They can be placed beneath low windows, or at book-case ends, or let into table tops or be specially-made free-standing fittings. The spines of the books lie at an angle of about 50° to the horizontal and the fitting may incorporate a small perpendicular display board on which a caption or notice can be placed.

The important thing to remember when displaying books, as distinct from book jackets, is that children should be allowed to borrow books straight away. It is frustrating to have one's interest in a book aroused and then discover that it cannot be borrowed until a particular day of the week. This practice is sometimes operated in order to inform as many people as possible about certain books, particularly new ones. Displaying book jackets is a better way of doing this.

Fig. 1. Bookcase with short shelves to take thin, tall books.

Fig. 2. Card catalogue with sloping drawers and sloping drawer pulls bearing only contents label holder. A groove beneath the drawer pulls enables the drawers to be pulled out. Not more than ten drawers would be required for any children's library. Most cabinets are made to order, from one drawer upwards.

Fig. 3. Wall slope to hold picture books for small children. Front covers are visible.

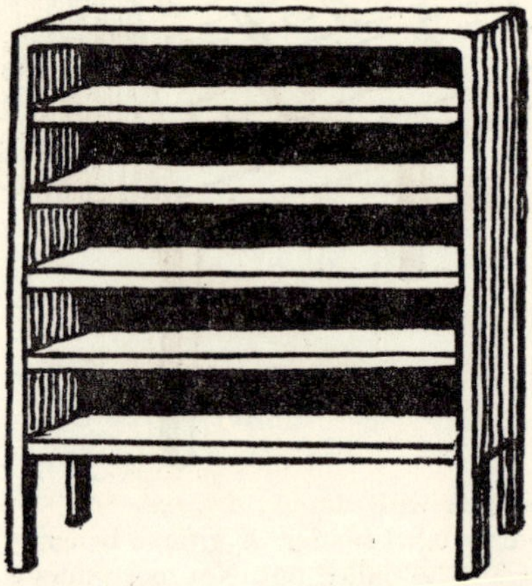

Fig. 4. Atlas and heavy volume case with shelves which slide out while the books are still on them to save wear on the bindings.

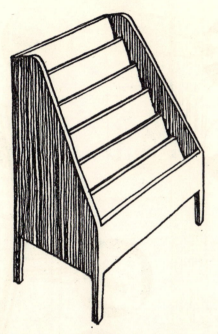

Fig. 5. Periodical display stand with sloping backs to prevent periodicals falling forward.

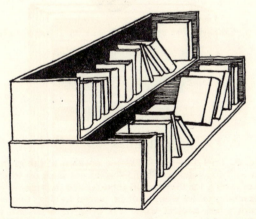

Fig. 6. Book box made in such a way that when unfastened the hinged lid will serve as a display shelf.

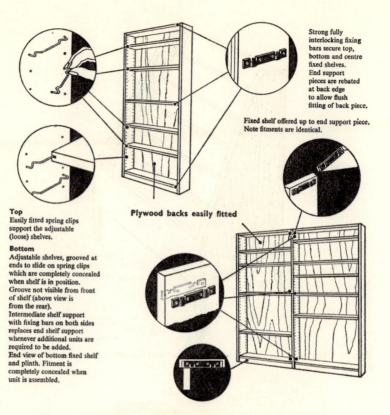

Strong fully interlocking fixing bars secure top, bottom and centre fixed shelves. End support pieces are rebated at back edge to allow flush fitting of back piece.

Fixed shelf offered up to end support piece. Note fitments are identical.

Top
Easily fitted spring clips support the adjustable (loose) shelves.

Bottom
Adjustable shelves, grooved at ends to slide on spring clips which are completely concealed when shelf is in position. Groove not visible from front of shelf (above view is from the rear).
Intermediate shelf support with fixing bars on both sides replaces end shelf support whenever additional units are required to be added.
End view of bottom fixed shelf and plinth. Fitment is completely concealed when unit is assembled.

Plywood backs easily fitted

Fig. 7. Construction assembly details for Lundia shelving.

Note on Fig. 8. This drawing shows the position of tables in relation to one another and to shelving. Chairs should not back on to shelves or on to the ends of tables, for they would then reduce passage-ways too much. In actual practice, tables would not be placed as close to one another as shown, except when project work was being undertaken, as it would restrict too much the space available for movement, and the room would be over crowded when busy.

Fig. 8. Arrangement of furniture in a children's library.

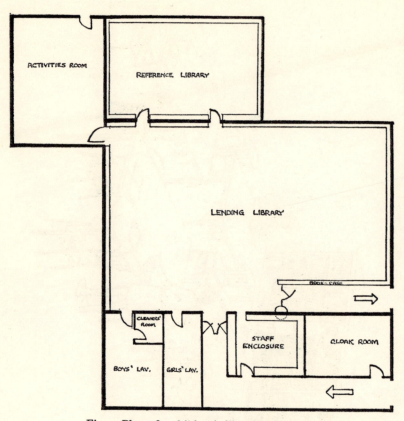

Fig. 9 Plan of a children's library suite.

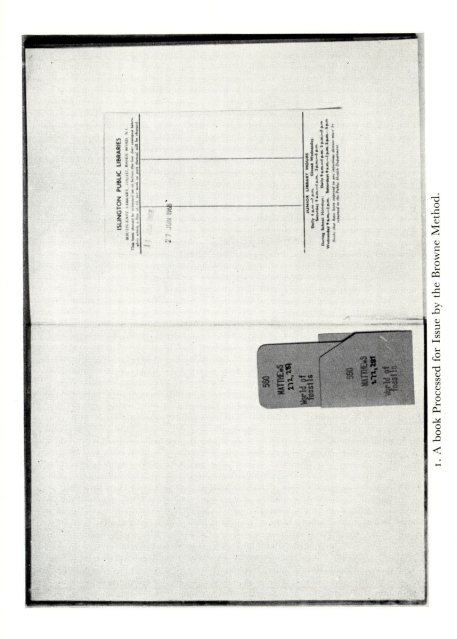

1. A book Processed for Issue by the Browne Method.

MAHONY, Bertha E [and others comp]

Illustrators of children... books, 1744-1945; compiled by Bertha E Mahony, Louise Payson Latimer, Beulah Folmsbee Boston (Mass.) Horn Book; London, Stevens + Brown. [1947]. illus bibliog.

028.5

MAHONY, Bertha B. and others comps.

Illustrators of children's books, 1744-1945; compiled by Bertha B. Mahony, Louise Payson Latimer, Beulah Folmsbee. Boston(Mass.), Horn Book; London, Stevens & Brown. [c1947]. illus. bibliog.

741.642
028.5

C
3

MAHONY, Bertha B. and others comps

Illustrators of children's books, 1744-1945; compiled by Bertha B. Mahony, Louise Payson Latimer, Beulah Folmsbee. Boston(Mass.), Horn Book; London, Stevens & Brown. [c1947]. illus. bibliog.

741.642
028.5

C
3

MAHONY, Bertha B. and others comps.

Illustrators of children's books, 1744-1945; compiled by Bertha B. Mahony, Louise Payson Latimer, Beulah Folmsbee. Boston(Mass.), Horn Book; London, Stevens & Brown. [c1947]. illus. bibliog.

741.642
028.5

C
3

2. Master Catalogue Entry and Copies of Entries Produced Therefrom by Means of a Spirit Duplicator.

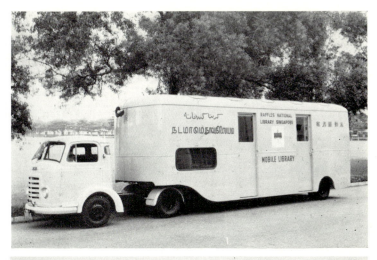

3, 4. Mobile Library, National Library, Singapore.

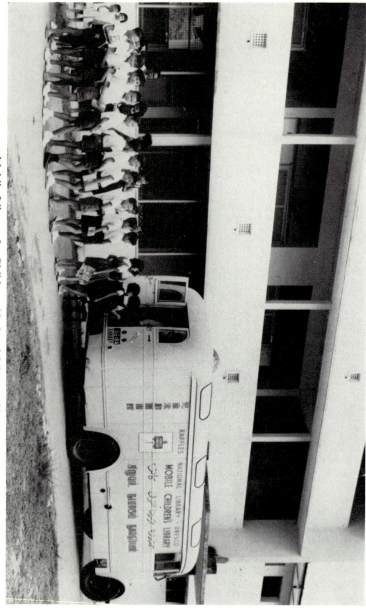

5. Mobile Library for Children, National Library, Singapore.

6. Children's Library, Clamart (Haute-de Seine), near Paris.

7, 8. Two views in the Children's Library, National Library, Singapore.

9. Lewis Carroll Library for Boys and Girls, Islington.

10. Mildmay Library, Islington.

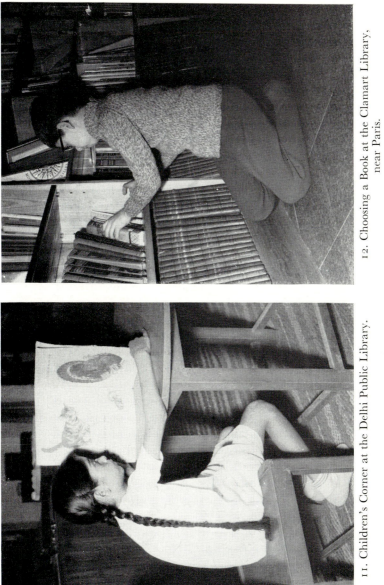

11. Children's Corner at the Delhi Public Library.

12. Choosing a Book at the Clamart Library, near Paris.

13, 14. Two Views in the Children's Library, Clamart, near Paris.

15. Tonks Strip and Stud for Adjustable Wooden Shelving.

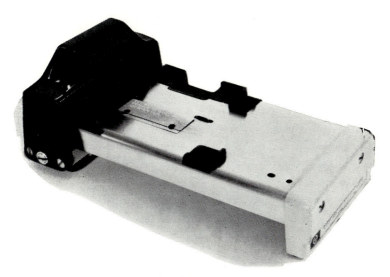

16. Name and Address Printing Machine.

17. Double Column Title-a-line Visible Index Panels.

Notes on Plates

PLATE 1. A large-page book emphasises the best position for the open-sided corner pocket which contains the book-card—close to the joint so that the book-card cannot fall out and be lost. It is desirable to have the times of opening on either the board label or the date label; the latter is better as times are apt to be changed and as date labels are replaced as they are filled up—but the board labels remain. When a board label (giving the name and address, or addresses, of the libraries and perhaps a few of the more important rules) is used, it is pasted above the corner pocket. Instead of a printed label, sometimes only the name of the library is rubber-stamped in this position.

PLATE 2. A spirit duplicator is a very useful piece of equipment in any library, but especially where several copies of a record are required. The entry in the top left-hand corner of the illustration is written by the cataloguer. The one below it is the master copy which is typed from it; the characters appear in reverse and bear a carbon deposit. The back of the typed paper has been photographed. It is from this master copy that all the other copies are made; those shown are the same, except the one at the top right-hand corner where both the class numbers (the one at which the book is classified and the added entry number) are shown. It will be noticed that both these appear on the master entry. By means of incising around the added entry number and the "C" indicating that the book is stocked in the Central Library on the master entry slip, it is possible to provide all, or only a selection, of the information typed on the "master". Added author, illustrator, or other headings can be entered on the "master" and similarly reproduced at will. If title entries are required then titles may be typed over the duplicated matter on the individual entry. If the typing on the master is carefully placed, it can also be used to reproduce the essential part, at any rate, of the information given in the catalogue entry on the book-card, whether it is made of manilla or of plastic. This saves the cutting of a special master (as was done in the case of the book illustrated in Plate 1) but it does mean that this information appears running up the card instead of across it. Additional copies of entries produced by the spirit duplicator can be used for accession, audit or other records, or for sending particulars of books added to stock to a union catalogue, or for compiling a list of additions or bibliography, etc. This is the main advantage of the spirit duplicator—providing multiple copies, which are all accurate, from one typing.

PLATES 3, 4. These photographs were taken before the name of the library was changed by the omission of the word "Raffles". The trailer is of the low loading type with small wheels; this results in the floor of the vehicle being quite close to the ground and so avoids a step or two. It also has a very low coupling device resulting in there being only one step inside the vehicle leading to the front part over the coupling device. The staff enclosure is placed between the doors. The books are not placed on shelves but in short aluminium trays so that when the vehicle returns to the headquarters, the stock can be changed completely in a very short time simply by taking the trays of books into the stands in the stock room and taking from the stands other trays containing a different type of book, maybe books for adults instead of for children, or of books in a different language for a village which is inhabited by people predominantly of another race. The rear door slides between the "skin" of the vehicle and the shelves as do the other doors. The upper half of it is a sliding window and permits through ventilation when the door is closed. If another vehicle is provided with a rear door in the right half instead of the left, both can be placed back to back and operated as one library. Provision is made to house a tape recorder and a gramophone turntable in the staff enclosure so that music and announcements can be broadcast through the amplifier visible at the front of the vehicle. In tropical countries the ventilation of such a vehicle is a problem. Small fans must be used to supplement natural ventilation; they may be activated by batteries or by plugging into electric street lighting standards.

PLATE 5. This mobile library was converted from a Royal Navy bus. It was purchased, adapted and equipped with a grant of money from Unesco which was made in order to demonstrate library work with children. It is used exclusively to carry books between schools and that is why it is possible to have a door at the rear as well as one on the left-hand side. When such vehicles wait alongside public roads it is unsafe for rear doors to be used.

PLATE 6. Round buildings are very expensive to construct; it is also very expensive to make wall shelving for them. The shelves in this library appear untidy largely because they are at different levels; also the absence of a top, or cornice, gives an unresolved, restless feeling. The artificial light fittings are obtrusive; it is very much more preferable, for light fittings to be built into ceilings, especially when they are low. The design of the furniture uses a method of construction which has the disadvantage that the bent legs are dust traps. Much contemporary furniture suffers from this disadvantage, and in some countries it is both expensive and difficult to find people to work as cleaners. The windows are placed in the best position for lighting the room, namely close to the ceiling. Light values decrease rapidly the lower the windows are. The sills are an appropriate distance above the wall shelving, and this prevents the glare which so often occurs when looking at books under windows into which the sun is shining.

PLATE 7. The bookcase is appropriately low so that the children can easily see and handle the books. Shelves are often so high that children cannot reach them or see the titles of those on the upper shelves. When the shelves are long and contain many thin books which tend to slide about because there are so many to each shelf, it is particularly important to see that they are not out of the reach of the children for whom they are intended. The condition of the books indicates a phase through which this relatively new library was temporarily passing when the photograph was taken. Sometimes a library's very popularity causes problems which cannot be dealt with quickly and adequately.

PLATE 8 shows shelving and a periodical fitting of appropriate height. The slope at the top of the bookcase on which the picture books are placed is at the right angle and the right height. One disadvantage of the periodical fitting is that the back above the top shelf appears to be perpendicular instead of sloping, with the result that a wire has to be placed in front of the periodicals to prevent them falling forwards. If they had been placed in periodical cases this would not have been necessary but such cases, especially those with plastic fronts, are expensive. Cane-seated chairs are most appropriate in tropical countries and can be made easily by local craftsmen; they can be just as easily reseated at little cost when necessary.

PLATE 9. The natural lighting is good in this building, the windows being placed as high as possible. The deep picture window gives those inside a choice of view and also enables those passing by to see into the library— in itself good publicity. A bench seat is very popular if placed under such a window. The deep window sill provides a place to display books. The room is not over-furnished (or to put it another way, the room is not congested even when well-used) and leaves room for extra chairs and tables to be brought in when a school class attends for project work. The chairs are upholstered and the tables have rounded corners and rounded edges at the outsides of the legs as all tables in libraries should have. Linoleum is let into the tops of the tables; this does not readily show wear, does not require maintenance (as does polished wood when subject to much use), and is easily replaced should this ever become necessary. It also has the great advantage that not being a shiny surface it does not reflect light.

PLATE 10. This is a one-room library, the children being allocated approximately one half of the room and the adults the other. There are several features worth observing. It is desirable, from an aesthetic point of view, in a one-room library for all the shelving to be of the same height; this is achieved, and at the same time the top shelf containing children's books are within reach of all but the smallest borrowers, by filling in the top shelf with a front which is hinged at the top and so providing storage space (always an eventual problem in a small library) for books, spare jackets and other display materials. It also provides a place for tier guides indicating the subjects of the books below. The counter in which the records of books on loan to children are kept is appropriately low. It is mounted on casters so that at busy periods it can be moved to provide a wider entrance thus enabling adults and children to be attended to at the same time without being in the same queue, the queues for adults and for children being back to back. At slack times the records of children's books on loan are kept in the main staff enclosure so that the staff can deal with the return of all books at the same place. The rather ugly gas heating fittings suspended from the ceiling are due to the fact that the library was constructed at a time of stringent restriction of expenditure on public buildings and it was therefore necessary to install a heating system that was inexpensive.

PLATE 11. The table shown here is rather tall for the girl using it, and it is high in relation to the chair. Also it has a top which is small in area; small tables are unsatisfactory in that they are inconvenient for four children to use at one time. Oblong and square tables are more suitable than round ones. Tables should be constructed without low rails connecting the legs; they are a nuisance in that they are in the way of the feet, and they become badly scratched. Such rails are provided to make the table rigid. This can be achieved by other means. The coconut matting is unsatisfactory in that dirt and dust which inevitably lodges between the fibres cannot be satisfactorily removed entirely, even with a vacuum cleaner.

PLATE 12. Large and very heavy books, as well as thin ones, are best kept on short shelves, otherwise they tend to slide and fall about easily, the large ones suffering damage by this means or as they are taken off the shelves. The adjustability of the shelves is limited; the holes in the uprights are placed in groups of three, and they are not placed as closely as is desirable.

PLATE 13. The boys are standing at adequately guided shelves, there being a subject guide on each. It is common practice to use a tier guide with a more embracing term for the subjects of all the books in the shelves below. Such specific guiding of the kind shown makes it frequently necessary to examine the guides in relation to the subjects of the books on the shelves or they become misleading.

PLATE 14. If a cloakroom is not provided with an attendant to look after the clothes, brief cases, baskets, etc. which are handed in, it is a good idea to provide shelves and coat hooks which the children can use. If this is done, there is, however, the risk that articles placed thereon may be stolen. Sensitive floor coverings are easily damaged by modern Western-type footwear, and in this library all persons entering have to remove their footwear and walk about in stockinged feet. In this particular library this is not a great discomfort as under-floor heating is provided. This form of heating is very uncomfortable for those who have to work for lengthy periods, and is expensive, save in those countries where electricity is very cheap.

PLATE 15. This is the original method of providing complete and close adjustability of shelving, and has been used in England for at least sixty years; it is still the most efficient for wooden shelving. Two strips are screwed over grooves on the sides of each of the uprights, and not further than 1″ from the edges, otherwise the shelves may tilt and the books fall off. These grooves are in order to take the back part of the studs after they have been inserted in slots in the strip. The studs have a point on which the shelves rest, and the weight of the books prevents the shelves sliding about. The slots in the strips are placed at intervals of ¾″.

PLATE 16. A machine which is used to print expendable slips bearing a borrower's name and address from embossed plastic membership cards as part of the Islington method of recording the loan of books. A dating device can be incorporated in such a machine if desired.

PLATE 17. Double-column title-a-line visible index panels are particularly suitable for the subject index to the classification, and for a list (for staff use) of books reserved. Panels can be fastened to a wall or catalogue, or placed on a fixed or revolving stand. The type illustrated takes two columns of 4″ strips, and the panels may be 12″ or 22″ long.

A Select Bibliography

I. LIBRARIES FOR CHILDREN — GENERAL

MCCOLVIN, LIONEL R. *Libraries for children*. Phoenix House. 1961.

Public library services for children. Unesco. (*Unesco Public Library Manuals*). 1957.

ROE, ERNEST *Teachers, librarians and children: a study of libraries in education*. Crosby Lockwood. 1965.

II. BOOK PRODUCTION

JENNETT, SEAN *The making of books*. 3rd ed. Faber. 1964.

MCMURTRIE, DOUGLAS C. *The book: the story and bookmaking*. O.U.P. 1943.

WILSON, R. N. D. *Books and their history shown to the children*. Nelson. 1930.

III. BOOKS FOR CHILDREN

BECKER, MAY LAMBERTON *Choosing books for children*. O.U.P. 1936.

CROUCH, MARCUS *Treasure seekers and borrowers*. Library Association. 1962.

CUTFORTH, J. A., *and* BATTERSBY, S. H. *Children and books*. Blackwell. 1962.

JENKINSON, A. J. *What do boys and girls read? An investigation into reading habits with some suggestions about the teaching of literature in secondary schools*. 2nd edition, with new appendix. Methuen. 1946.

LEWIS, NAOMI, *compiler*. *The best children's books of 1967*. Hamilton. 1968.

LINES, KATHLEEN, *compiler*. *Four to fourteen*. 2nd ed. National Book League. 1956.

NATIONAL BOOK LEAGUE, *Have you read this? A wide range of books for parents, teachers and librarians to read and consider suggesting to teenagers*. [An annotated list of 435 titles.] 1967. *School library books: non-fiction*. 2nd ed. 1968.

SAUNDERS, W. L., *compiler. A guide to book lists and bibliographies for the use of school librarians. 2nd ed. rev. and enl.* School Library Association. 1961.

SCHOOL LIBRARY ASSOCIATION *Books of reference for school libraries: an annotated list based on the 4th ed. of 'A list of general reference books' with some additional material on school subjects and children's leisure interests.* Rev. ed. 1968.

Eleven to fifteen: a basic book list of non-fiction for secondary school libraries. Compiled by PEGGY HEEKS. 3rd ed. rev. and enl. 1963.

Books for primary children. Edited by Berna Clark. 3rd ed. of *Primary school library books.* 1968.

TREASE, GEOFFREY *Tales out of school.* Heineman. 1948.

TURNER, E. S. *Boys will be boys.* Michael Joseph. 1948.

WHITE, DOROTHY NEAL *About books for children.* Published for the New Zealand Library Association by Whitcombe & Tombs and O.U.P. 1946.

For other Books, see pages 63–64.

INDEX

Compiled by L. M. Harrod

Illustrations are given in italics except for plates: these are indicated by Pl. followed by the plate number. Indexed matter in the notes on the plates is given by the page number followed by the plate number thus: 206 (Pl. 6).